# DANCING FOR A LIVING

A Career in the World of Dance

# My Life and My Work Series

My Life and My Work Series
edited by Rachel Bleackley

# DANCING FOR A LIVING

## ballet and contemporary dance

by Hilary Cartwright

with a foreword by Peter Brinson

**Educational Explorers · Reading**

*First published* 1974
© *Hilary Cartwright* 1974
isbn 0 85225 755 4

*Published by Educational Explorers Limited*
*40 Silver Street, Reading, England*
*Set in 'Monotype' Bembo and printed in Great Britain by*
*Hazell Watson & Viney Limited, Aylesbury, Bucks*

# CONTENTS

# ACKNOWLEDGEMENT

*The Author and the Publisher gratefully acknowledge
the kind help and advice given by*

THE ROYAL ACADEMY OF DANCING

THE ROYAL BALLET

*and*

THE LONDON SCHOOL OF CONTEMPORARY DANCE

*and are indebted to the following for permission to
publish the illustrations in this book*

JOE BANGAY

ANTHONY CRICKMAY

ZOE DOMINIC

HELEN LEOUSSI

LONDON CONTEMPORARY DANCE THEATRE

ROY ROUND

THE ROYAL BALLET

MICHAEL STANNARD

REG WILSON

# ILLUSTRATIONS

Inset at pages 61 to 68

# FOREWORD

*by*

PETER BRINSON
*Director, Calouste Gulbenkian Foundation*
*Lisbon, United Kingdom and British Commonwealth Branch*

ALL OVER THE WORLD at this moment people concerned with training professional dancers or would-be dancers are discussing a problem affecting the whole nature of how and what a dancer learns. It concerns the amount of time which should be given to technical training (the learning of steps, classroom exercises and so on) and the time which should be given to general education, including what extra knowledge of music, painting and cultural history a dancer should have. In other words, how to train artists and human beings who think for themselves, rather than just technicians who can spin like tops but never ask or wonder why!

I remember opening a dance education conference in Canada last summer with just this theme. Earlier this year the Gulbenkian Foundation in London devoted a lot of time to the same question at another dance conference of top teachers. It is difficult to strike the right balance because even the technical side of a dancer's training today is so demanding it could easily occupy all a young person's waking hours if we are not very careful.

So when I came to read Hilary Cartwright's personal story of the dancing career I was fascinated to see how much she emphasises her importance of acquiring interests outside dancing and how valuable to her own success was the broad cultural education she was given during her training at Elmhurst Ballet School. 'Distractions act like a holiday', she says. 'Dancers need to see the rest of life.'

This approach emphasises the immense value of having a career book written by someone who has actually lived the life. Ballet, after all, is not all glamour and joy. It's also grinding hard work, loneliness, despair. The important thing is to know at the beginning you're going to have to overcome the difficult side to achieve the rewards of the other. Once you accept this, things fall into the right perspective. Here, in Hilary's book, is the feeling and the truth of the matter.

She *knows* (because she's done it!) the importance of a knowledge of acting to success on stage for a dancer; what a fight it is to correct the small physical defects most of us have so as to make the most of our bodies; and how to face the heartbreak of injury. Apart from all the useful tips about touring, diet, costumes, make-up and other things which Hilary Cartwright recalls, her book is exceptional for quite another quality of its author's experience. She not only made a successful career in the Royal Ballet, dancing important leading roles like Queen of the Wilis in *Giselle*, she also had to face the problem of early retirement and making another career in a way likely to face perhaps 50% of all those who become dancers, including many who will read this book.

Here her own wide interests and cultural education came to the rescue, plus toughness of character and a determination not to let things get her down. Granted she's a rarity in the dancing world, having literary as well as physical skill. But this extra experience gives us the bonus of finding out how she coped with unemployment, discovering the place of Equity and trade unionism in an artist's life and what other opportunities the world of theatre can offer as a career besides dancing.

The other thing I like about this book, beyond the breadth of its experience and the fact that all the advice it contains springs from that experience, is its loyalty to the dancing profession. Again loyalty is tempered by experience. She loves dancing and teaching dancing without being dewy-eyed about them. She is

practical without over-dedication; sensible without being patron-
ising; serious always with a touch of humour.

Come to think of it, these are the qualities needed by everyone
who hopes to be a dancer. Hilary Cartwright shows the reason
why.

PETER BRINSON
London

# I

## FACING FACTS

WHENEVER ANYONE LEARNS that I have been a dancer, almost invariably their first remark is either 'How wonderful, it must be such a marvellous life and so exciting' or 'You must be *so* fit'. To a degree both assumptions are quite correct, but I do also wonder how on earth I can begin to explain what a dancer's life is really like, and what a physical wreck one usually feels!

It has always seemed appalling to me, that the life and work one has chosen, should from necessity be so demanding, and become such an obsession that it excludes participation in anything else. Unfortunately dancing, and ballet in particular, can be just such a career, although the longer I remain connected with this profession the more I try to evade the grasping, octopus-like tentacles that threaten to enclose it.

This may seem a surprising comment from someone who has spent the majority of her life within the profession, and you are probably wondering why on earth I have continued to stay associated with it for so long. I can only say that there exists a strange love/hate relationship in every dancer's life, which it is impossible to eradicate, and whereby the loving always seems to be strongest.

I would not change the life I lead for any other. At the same time I would not actively encourage anyone else to follow a career in dance unless they are already well aware of the sort of life they are about to embark on. The work is challenging, creative, exciting, physically and morally demanding. But once you have acknowledged the threat of obsession in dance for what it is, to combat it is relatively simple. The problem for most young dancers, is recognising that there are inherent dangers in such a seemingly glamorous profession.

Frequently it is only the glamour of a dancer's life which is revealed, while the drudgery, sweat, tears and boredom are either politely swept beneath the carpet, or dramatised to the point of absurdity. I would like to lift rather more than the corner of this particular carpet, without exaggerating its murky aspect in any way, to try to let you see what is really involved in becoming a dancer.

So, no over-dramatisation in either direction, but merely an account of the sort of things that happened in my life—which are fairly typical of most dancers' ups and downs. In this way I hope you can be warned in advance, and can prevent some of the saddest and most heart-breaking disillusionments later on. Perhaps you will also see how the roof of your world need not collapse, should you be incapable of fulfilling your greatest ambitions.

Possibly the biggest enemy in any profession, or indeed any life-style, is narrow-mindedness, and the danger of becoming over-absorbed in the world of dance cannot be stressed too much. Eventually it can prove inhibiting in your work, and limiting to personal development. The natural curiosity we all of us have, can be a useful ally, and not an irritating distraction, for you may well find that if it is left to wander naturally and at random, it can help to prevent you from becoming too involved in the immediate environment of the ballet world: a world which seems to demand a very singular devotion at times.

The reputation ballet has for imposing a somewhat monastic discipline on your way of life is really exaggerated. Although a strict discipline is required, anything more rigorously self-enforced amounts to an excessive sense of dedication to one's art. Admirable as a sense of dedication may be, and very necessary to some extent, like all good things it can be carried too far. In the end you become a martyr to the gluttony of self-deprivation, and this is not at all an admirable trait. Arthur Rubinstein, the great concert pianist, once admitted to having such an

indefatigable curiosity and love of the world and its people
that he would occasionally neglect his daily practice in favour of
enjoying the sheer pleasure of living. He is now an octogenarian
whose work is still recognised as having the imagination and joy
of youthful discovery. An achievement which only comes from
remaining open to new ideas and opinions. I would never
suggest that any student should actually shirk his classes in training, but I am sure you will find that by exploring all the other
things in life, you too will gain an extra dimension in your work.

Primarily the world around you is most likely to be connected
with all the creative arts, like music, art, drama, painting and
literature. These have a profound effect upon the work you do,
for it is through their contributory influences that you become
more aware of the overall possibilities to be accomplished in
your work. I know I have always found the people and work
of these different yet similar media a refreshing and rewarding
source of inspiration. Invariably there is something new and
stimulating in what they have to offer, and one is prevented from
settling into a routine way of life, confined only to the world
of ballet.

Secondly, apart from the close impact of the artistic world,
there is of course the everyday world of social, economic, and
political activity, from which none of us can escape entirely. In
fact if you were made to, you would very soon miss it. There
is no need to become intensely political, but even a day without
newspapers is enough to make one realise how subconciously
we are all dependent on outside news and affairs. Certainly the
social aspect is not one to be avoided either. A life without
friends other than your dance colleagues eventually becomes
increasingly depressing and oppressive.

Initially one feels life is very much less complicated when you
have nothing else to think about but your work, and you can
give your undivided attention to it. I found very soon though,
that this comparatively negative attitude towards life had unpleasant repercussions. Without any outside activities there was
nothing to provide the occasional healthy distraction from work,

and distractions act like a holiday. You are mentally refreshed by the change, and apart from helping to put things more in perspective, you can approach your work with greater clarity.

This attitude ultimately results in your making better progress, although it is not always easy to find the right balance. One may go wildly plunging off at a tangent in both directions, with equally catastrophic results. Eventually most of us manage to find a fairly equable level, but a lot depends on the individual when deciding how much social life can be enjoyably combined with a conscientious approach to work. There are no hard and fast rules that can be learned or applied, for the balance must always depend on the amount of stamina you personally have to cope with the physical and mental demands made on you by ballet.

This really could be classed as the Number One problem in life, and yet it is never properly presented to students when they start to train seriously. It probably causes more distress and mis-understanding than anything else. No-one wants to forego a social life, and relationships with other people, especially when you are young. But ballet imposes its discipline beyond the classroom if you really want to take it up professionally, and it takes a lot of understanding both of yourself and from those around you to make life as satisfying and complete as it should be.

Maybe one of the first questions you should ask yourself while still a student is, 'Why am I dancing?' The answers are numerous. Ideally, as a profession, for you it is the only way you can creatively fulfil your purpose in life. Perhaps though, you enjoy it purely as a form of release for your emotions; or it is a more pleasurable activity than ordinary sports; or it could be a satisfying extension in movement of your other artistic talents; or it might merely represent an enjoyable hobby which you acquired through the physiotherapy treatment originally pre-scribed for some childhood illness or disability such as asthma, knock-knees, or weak ankles!

But you need to know which is the right answer for you. And because self-deception only leads to painful crises at a later date when a change of thought and career is twice as difficult, you constantly have to ask yourself the same question until you are sure of the true answer. If you are still uncertain and decide to give it a chance though, try to do so with your eyes open and prepare a second string to your bow. It will then be ready and waiting should you need it.

I feel at this point I should really try and dispel some of the gloom these harsh words must have cast on your enthusiasm. I have rather obscured the pleasures and rewards of being a dancer in my efforts to clarify some of these penalties which are usually ignored. I know that I personally could not have chosen a more satisfying or creative outlet for myself, which has led to an even more varied and interesting life as time goes by.

It is surely logical therefore to assume that what has applied to me and to many others in the past should continue to apply in the future. (It would certainly be a very sorry day for ballet if it did not!). So it may very well be right for you too. I hope I can show you some of the fun and enjoyment as well as the hardships, so you can decide for yourself whether this is a life that appeals to your idea of a satisfying and complete career.

# 2

## EARLY DAYS IN TRAINING AND DISCIPLINE

I HAVE ALWAYS FELT that I was very fortunate to attend a stage-school from an early age. Elmhurst Ballet School, in Camberley, combined both the educational and theatrical work very successfully. The training there left one in no doubt at all about the rigorous life ahead, and the discipline necessary in order to succeed. I have always been very grateful for such a basic and hard grounding, for it proved invaluable when I first started work professionally.

It was more by chance than choice that I went to Elmhurst. My sister, who is four years older than I, had already spent a year as an associate student at the junior section of the Royal Ballet School. At the end of the year, aged eleven, she was told she would grow too tall for classical ballet, which ultimately proved to be correct as she is now five foot nine inches. My parents were recommended to send her to Elmhurst where the training was more comprehensive and would prepare her for the commercial theatre without neglecting to give her a sound ballet background.

As Elmhurst was some seven or eight miles from where we lived, it seemed practical that I should go there as well. I had attended ballet classes from the age of three and enjoyed them tremendously. We also had a family tradition of 'dressing-up', which, apart from being great fun, was a marvellous outlet for excess energy on a winter's day. I was not aware of any particular desire actually to perform at the time, except that I sometimes wished I could prove that my efforts need not always provoke quite so much laughter! This frustration though may well have sowed the seeds of my appreciation of, and desire to aspire to the more romantic roles later on.

I started at my new school quite happily when I was seven, continuing to dance in a general class held once a week for less serious students in the junior school. Something began to stir inside me though, surrounded as I was by the enthusiastic atmosphere of the school and the more serious, consistent approach of my friends to their one-hour dancing class a day. By the time I was eight, I managed to convince my mother that I too should learn dancing full-time.

The dancing classes, although categorised separately from one's school work class, were still confined to age groups. I was fortunate to be placed in one that included the more advanced section of my age group. A fact which, even at that early age, did much to boost my morale and help convince me that I had made the right decision. There was little ill-feeling in the school about this system of grading, for in spite of the naturally keen sense of competition, we all got on surprisingly well.

We learned to accept, as a matter of fact, that because of various circumstances beyond one's control, some people appear to have a better start in life than others. At the same time we were also taught that through hard work and determination, anyone could achieve the same results in the long run.

I had one very good friend who had the advantage (or so I felt) of coming from a theatrical background. Imogen and I have remained firm friends, and I remember how surprised I was later, to discover that we had *both* benefited from the differences in our backgrounds. She enjoyed the comparative peace of our home-life and coming with us on typical family holidays, while I certainly was enthralled by the contrast of her home-life.

There was the awe-inspiring yet kindly figure of her father, Christopher Hassall, who must never be disturbed once he retired to his study to write, no matter what emergency might occur; while her mother, a delightful ex-actress and singer was as lively and energetic as her children. And then there were all the theatrical friends of the family who I had admired from a distance and who seemed to be encountered on every outing. It was more than enough to convince me that I too wanted to be in the theatre.

It was not until many years later though that I was to decide it was dancing in preference to any other facet of a stage career, that was to be my goal, for at Elmhurst there was an equal stress on acting and ballet. The class with which I danced was the same as the one with which I acted, so the competition in both areas was on equal levels and the choice remained open for a long time. We were also made very aware of how important each is to the other, for an actress needs to know how to move, and a dancer how to act.

Poetry recitations were also a part of our education programme, and once a year a few students were approved to stand before the visiting examiner for the Poetry Lovers Fellowship. In order to qualify, and as a final seal of approval, one had to audition to the headmistress in her private sitting room. A truly terrifying ordeal, as she was an awesome woman of majestic bearing and great quality.

Helen Mortimer really was a magnificent person, and greatly respected by the theatrical profession and her pupils alike. However at the age of seven, when I had never actually been face to face with her before, my first experience of this trial run recital was shattering, as well as being an initiation into the agonies of off-stage nerves. The memory of this particular sensation has always remained with me very forcibly.

I waited to be summoned, shivering from head to foot with nerves outside her door. At last the time came. First of all my knuckles refused to make contact with the door for the customary knock before entering. I seemed to have no strength at all, and my knees were visibly shaking. Once inside worse was to follow. I handed over the two pieces I had prepared, and immediately my mind went blank.

Fortunately Helen Mortimer was very understanding, and helped me over my humiliation by suggesting that perhaps if I went outside the door where I had known the poems a few moments ago, I might remember them again. I admired the logic of this remark, duly went out, only to return at once with a perfect recollection of the poems. How I wished in later years that there could be opportunities for a second chance to perform—once one had recovered from the initial shock of contact with the audience.

The school's almost non-stop productions soon taught me that weak nerves had to be mastered in order to get on. These performances were another valuable part of my training, for with a steady annual output ranging from pure ballet through variety to dramatic plays, we became familiar with many of the intricacies and various 'hoodoos' of stage procedure. And of course gained some of the experience and confidence required for performing.

It was not until I was about twelve that I began to show any technical ability in my dancing. In many ways this was not surprising, for it is usually about this age that the real challenge in ballet begins to make itself felt. Up until this age, a child's body is much more malleable and supple; and dancing is really just another immensely enjoyable form of exercise and recreation.

There are of course steps to be learned and the desire to accomplish them as pleasingly as possible. But as the body begins to set into your inherent physique so the real battle with your body begins. A certain amount may have been achieved to combat bow-legs, knock-knees, flat feet or a weak spine if the early training has been carefully supervised, but unless you are exceptionally lucky there will always be some physical defect—however slight it may appear superficially—which will become your personal bugbear for the rest of your career.

You may have very narrow hips, which can restrict your degree of turn out, or terribly knobbly knees which never look *quite* straight, though you may feel as though you are forcing your knee caps through the back of your legs! It is only if you feel you have the determination to overcome any of these physical disadvantages, and are prepared to work extremely hard towards perfecting all your current repertoire of steps, as well as learning those that are more complicated and advanced, that it is worth continuing with ballet at this stage.

The enjoyment and pleasure of dancing, which buoyed you up

as a child will, of course, still remain. But the hard physical endurance of future training will make extra heavy demands unless you are prepared to face them.

It is also about this time that girls start pointe work. Despite the agony this is bound to cause, I know most young girls cannot wait to clamber into a pair of pointe shoes. One staggers around in an elated fashion feeling that any day now you are going to emerge as the future *ballerina assoluta*. Disillusionment however follows hard on the heels of this initial state of euphoria, and the realities of getting up on *pointe*, and staying there, becomes literally painfully obvious. I must admit though, my rather square-ended feet stood me in good stead, providing a fairly natural platform, and I was really able to enjoy pointe work without suffering too much.

I also had an averagely high instep, which was strong enough to support the foot on *pointe*, rather than a cripplingly overdeveloped instep which pushes the foot over the *pointe* too far. The main thing to remember about pointe work is never to be afraid of it. After all there is only approximately another eight inches to fall, if all does not go according to plan. And it's a marvellous feeling once you have mastered what really amounts to a sort of knack, superimposed on the basic classical technique.

It was about this time that I started to study for my Elementary exam. We were only entered for the major Royal Academy of Dancing Examinations at Elmhurst, which was a very wise policy. Too many people stake their hopes on a future career in ballet based on minor examinations results, which are really only an assessment by one or two people of whether you have reached a required standard.

Their judgement cannot be a wholly reliable indication of your actual talent. The verdict can err equally in both directions. And that is why, in my opinion, all exams although providing a goal to work towards, do not offer any sort of guide towards the actual possibilities of a serious career in dancing.

A point always worth remembering throughout your training is that during the earlier years of your life your whole personality is undergoing constant emotional and physical changes. A dancer who can be very promising up to the age of fourteen of fifteen, may very often not progress beyond this point. The mature artist never develops from this chrysalis, but always remains on the brink of becoming something.

That person has then exhausted his potential as a dancer, and all the glowing reports and exam results will not provide the assurance a company manager needs when engaging dancers. Late developers on the other hand may have talent which has lain dormant throughout their youth, waiting for the moment in their development when it can satisfactorily blossom into life.

At the moment though exams are still a necessary evil to some extent, in order to place yourself in a position of qualified acceptability, in an already overcrowded profession. The only other thing to be said in their favour is that, if you have not had the opportunity of appearing in front of an audience, they do at least give you some idea of how easy it is for your legs to turn to water, completely refusing to obey you at the crucial moment.

Although not too great an importance was placed on these exams at Elmhurst, the fact that I did do particularly well when I took my Elementary, meant that the opportunities and openings to improve and broaden my dancing and acting were actively encouraged instead of being merely observed. It also meant that I had proved how hard work and determination can achieve results, regardless of the advantages or disadvantages you may start with. The rather odd disadvantage I had started with was being a day-girl. We were never quite sure why this should be so, but I can only imagine that because we were not on the premises all the time, we did not appear to be so involved in the school activities as the boarders.

Another close friend, also a day-girl, who went on to succeed on the acting side was Jennifer Hilary. She eventually graduated to R.A.D.A. where she won the Gold Medal, and went on to a successful acting career. We formed a close alliance through this mutual struggle, and were able to bolster each other's courage whenever things looked particularly black.

Having managed to pass the initial weeding out process, when those who had shown no positive signs of suitablity for a theatrical career were advised to change schools, the pressure of work really began to mount. On entering the senior part of the school at twelve or thirteen, we started to work towards the G.C.E. exams, which came at the end of the third year, so educationally the pressure increased.

Previously we had received one hour of ballet six days a week. The majority of the training we were doing was ballet, but it also included one character, one modern, and one limbering class each week, with probably an additional hour in the evening three times a week for work towards exams. Now we practised every evening, doing two hours together sometimes.

In addition there were the termly shows. These involved extra rehearsals which had to be squeezed into Saturdays, and even longer evening periods. Not everyone was in all of them, as you will see, but by the time I was fourteen, I and several of my contemporaries were involved in most of them, which made a fairly heavy schedule.

It had its compensations though, for the actual excitement and thrill of performing more than made up for all the hard work beforehand. We were basically a very happy school, and although we were taught the hard part of theatre life, we were also shown the fun and sense of achievement that can be produced through combined efforts.

The Christmas term had two events. First there was a large complex production, which was mainly balletic, with a substantial amount of acting to carry the thread of the story. This was performed in a theatre to the public over a period of two weeks, and the proceeds were sent to a charity. The second was a version of the Christmas story, performed in the School Chapel, again to the public. Although this play was the same each year it nearly always involved learning a new part, which never dulled its repetition, and even returning to familiar parts was just as rewarding.

We performed it with the same pleasure and affection each year, and I was to find in later years that a similar feeling exists in ballet companies for certain favourite ballets. It's rather like shrugging on an old overcoat which has become a familiar friend when you return to a role or ballet that always manages to retain its initial youth and substance.

In the Easter term everyone had to present a choreographic solo work, lasting two to three minutes. The idea had to be devised entirely individually, suitable music found, a costume designed and made, and rehearsal time arranged with one of the School's pianists. I found these agonising to do and by the end of ten years new ideas were becoming increasingly thin on the ground! But they were undoubtedly good experience.

Accompanying these choreographic efforts were two ballet solos arranged by Helen Fisher, the Dance Principal, one for the juniors and one for the seniors. Six finalists were chosen from each section following a day of preliminary viewing by Helen Fisher and the rest of the dancing staff. A visiting adjudicator from the professional ballet world, would then present the much prized silver cups to the winner of each group. Following this, two one-act plays were presented towards the end of term, and an Easter Play which was performed in the School Chapel. The School was, and I believe still is, very High Church which accounts for so much religious activity.

Finally in the Summer term, a production by the 'Mortimer Minors' started the ball rolling. This was a light-hearted revue, created mainly by its participants, with the acts they had devised, produced and polished into shape by Helen Fisher, who also provided any additional material when necessary. We had to audition to her in order to be accepted into the Group, either individually or with friends, by presenting a ready made song and dance act or a monologue.

These auditions were held once or twice a year, and even when you were in the Group you had to re-audition each time. It was far worse than any professional commercial enterprise, for you never knew whether you were going to be kept in the group or not. But somehow this element of chance made re-acceptance an even more treasured triumph.

The poetry exams came next, and lastly the end-of-year Demonstration. This was performed to our parents after the prize-giving ceremony on the last day of term. While they sat in a marquee erected on a grass tennis court, we performed on an adjoining grass court some two feet higher, using the surrounding bushes and shrubs as wings for exits and entrances. An example of classroom work at varying age levels, was followed by a more lyrical set of costumed dances based on a central theme.

So it was a fairly active year, especially when re-making, mending and altering the costumes was the responsibility of the older girls. Fortunately anyone over the age of nine had to launder and iron their own costumes, but it still meant keeping your own in good condition, and you soon learned that costumes had to be hung up immediately they were taken off, and not just flung in a heap on the floor.

This became a habit which stuck in later years, when I was in the Company and there were dressers to help hang up costumes. It was a small help to another constantly over-worked department of the theatre, and I was horrified at the lack of care many people showed towards costly garments which they just left lying on the floor, in the expectation that someone else would pick them up.

There is really no room for that sort of arrogance in the theatre. No-one should be expected to wait on anyone else, for each of us has a job to do and co-operation all round helps to make any company operate more smoothly and happily.

Another department of the theatre which I learned to respect and admire from my school-day experiences was the workshop and its staff. We had to paint and make the majority of the scenery for each production, and I can remember sitting up until nearly midnight in my final year endeavouring to stitch two halves of a heavy plastic laminated backcloth together on a sewing machine.

I was aided and abetted by two friends, one of whom was Diana Fox (now Diana Vere and a principal with the Royal Ballet.) Abetted was the more accurate term, for when it was complete we found we had stitched one of the two pieces together upside down. Our reaction was weak and helpless laughter and the hope that, being a fairly abstract design, no-one would notice! Needless to add, of course they did, and we had to do it all again. Nothing it seems is easy in the theatre.

The most menial task in any job is sweeping the floor. At Elmhurst we swept the studios. This was worked on a rota which usually meant doing it two or three times a week, first thing in the morning. These studios were not the height of luxury then either. The floors were reasonable although a little splintery; there was a mirror at the end of each studio and the heating was minimal. So much so that we had to wear fur gloves in the winter sometimes for although warm inside from working, the extremities were nipped by icy draughts whistling through the windows and between floorboards.

The studios were scattered through the woods in the grounds of the School and were built of wooden slats with asbestos roofing. Indeed, one was known as the hen-house, because of the flap down insets in one wall in place of windows, which made it look like a chicken coop in the summer. There have been vast improvements since I left in 1960, although even I managed to perform in the then newly built School theatre.

After taking and passing seven G.C.E. subjects I stayed on for a further year studying art, drama, music and of course ballet. Our dancing was increased to five or six hours a day in order to gain strength and confidence before auditioning for the Royal Ballet School. I did not really know for sure that ballet was to be the career for me until I and two others had actually been accepted by the Royal Ballet School following the audition.

I knew that it was what *I* most wanted to do. But the opinion of those who taught me was that, although I was technically quite good, I did not seem to have the temperament for really classical work. I was considered of a lightweight nature more suited to the all-round work required for the commercial theatre. I was obviously one of the late developers, but the encouragement of being accepted by the Royal Ballet School made me feel it was worth pursuing my dream.

So in the end the final decision was taken for me, and I was no longer torn between deciding whether I should act or dance, or both!

I should also like to add that it is not absolutely essential to attend a school similar to Elmhurst or White Lodge (the junior school attached to the Royal Ballet School) in order to succeed as a professional dancer, or even to be eligible to enter the Royal Ballet Senior School. Many dancers have had a far less favourable start to their careers without it proving to be a disadvantage in any way.

So if the possibility of your attending a specialist school is slight, do not feel you stand any the less chance of proving your capabilities as a dancer. Many dancers attend normal day-school and go to outside studios for dancing classes about twice or three times a week. All major towns have at least one school of dancing run by recognised teachers where an adequate training for entry to the Royal Ballet School can be gained. (See the appendix for more detailed information.)

It may also be of interest to note that since September 1973, White Lodge has come directly under the Department of Education and Science. This means that parents with limited incomes pay only a minimal amount towards the total fees, based on a related incomes policy. Anyone who has the talent therefore can go to the Royal Ballet's junior school irrespective of their background, or the part of Britain in which they live.

# 3

## GROUNDWORK FOR GRADUATION

IN MANY WAYS it was initially something of a disappointment when we finally reached the Royal Ballet School. We had expected an increase in work rather than a decrease, but we had not realised how lucky we had been in our last year at Elmhurst. Working in a much smaller community, and in a class consisting of five people, we were able to receive virtually individual attention throughout the day. Now, at the 'Royal', we had on average only two classes a day in groups of twenty to thirty students. One class every day was classical. The other varied, and was devoted to either mime, character, virtuosity or repertory.

Mime consisted of learning the traditional language of the classical mime as used in the nineteenth century ballet classics. It is difficult to trace this form of mime back to any one source, for it draws a great deal from both the pantomime of the *Commedia dell'Arte*, as well as the classical mime language of the Greek and Roman tragedies, which eventually became known as the *Atellenae*. The movements have to be very clearly executed in order to convey the meaning to an audience unfamiliar with the language of this sort of mime.

There are set movements to describe 'a handsome young man', 'a beautiful young girl', a 'King', a 'Queen', 'money', 'work', and so on. These specific movements developed as the *Commedia dell'Arte* artists, who wore masks depicting the characters they were playing, depended upon gestures of their hands rather than expression of their faces to indicate the emotions and plot of the scenario they were acting.

An interesting sidelight when learning the manner in which

to link together the sequence of mime actions is that one becomes aware that the verb invariably comes at the end of a sentence, exactly as it does in Latin grammar. For instance, in the *Sleeping Beauty* Prologue, the Fairies arriving at the Court have to mime, 'I here the baby bless. I here the baby bring ★ ★ ★ ★ ★' whatever the gift each Fairy has brought.

Similarly in *Swan Lake* Act IV, the two big Swans mime to the distraught Swan Queen, 'You here die not, I you save'. All of which is really rather awkward to remember, and can be very confusing and obscure to the audience. I do not think that many people realise in Act II *Swan Lake* that the Swan Queen, in the story she tells the Prince, shows him that the lake on which she swims is filled with her mother's tears!

It is amazing how careful and precise one has to be with each gesture; and it takes a great deal of patient practice to become a good mime artist. Unfortunately it is an art which is vastly underestimated on the whole by most ballet students, who do not recognise its value, both in perpetuating the classical tradition in mime, as well as providing valuable groundwork on which to base other less rigidly disciplined mime actions.

We learned several mime passages from the classics during these classes, as well as learning to use the mime language in our own improvised stories. In this way we learned how much the rest of the body, as well as the hands and face had to be used to convey the actions with any strength of meaning. It is incredibly hard to tell a story, which can be understood by other people, without resorting to words at all; as you may have already discovered in playing a simple game of charades.

Character, meant studying the national dances of the Eastern and Mid-European countries as well as the more familiar Spanish Flamenco or Italian Tarantellas. We learned the style and character of the true national dances of Poland, Czechoslovakia and Hungary, which were mainly Czardas and Mazurka rhythms, as well as the more stylized balletic versions of these national dances.

These balletic versions, as used in *Swan Lake* Act III for example, are still relatively authentic, but have a more delicate approach than the earthy robustness of the true peasant dances. This sort of adaptation is very typical of the style and approach adopted by the choreographers of the late nineteenth century. The story of *Don Quixote* is another pastiche, this time, of a Spanish dance, and although very attractive and exciting to watch, can hardly be termed authentic, as it involves a considerable amount of pointe work.

It is really no more uncommendable a procedure though than a composer who takes the peasant songs and music of a country to form the basis of a piece of music. Stravinsky many times based a score on old Russian folk songs or melodies, and they have never been considered any the worse for this.

We wore heeled character shoes for these classes, as the nature of the work is too hard on the feet when they are clad only in soft ballet shoes. Also the majority of these dances are performed, if not in high boots, at least in a similar sort of hard leather shoe with a raised heel.

Virtuosity, a strange sounding name for a class, literally meant learning steps and variations of virtuoso standards.

The class was entirely on *pointes* and consisted of learning the solo variations from classical ballets. This gave us a superior standard to work towards, without being just a series of class room exercises. We were also able to appreciate that what looked relatively simple when performed on stage, was in fact a most exacting and tiring piece to dance.

Finally, the repertory class was again directly connected with Company work, for we learned the *corps de ballet* work from the repertoire currently being performed. This was done for two reasons. Firstly, it gave us some idea of what it was like to work in a group of people, where uniformity took precedence over individualism, and secondly, it prepared us for going into the company itself, by providing us with some knowledge of the work we would have to learn initially. Always supposing any of us would be accepted!

# 4

## POLISHING AND PREPARING FOR THE
## PROFESSIONAL LIFE

A LARGE NUMBER OF THE STUDENTS of the Royal Ballet School have their fees paid by local authorities, as distinct from others whose fees are paid privately, say by parents. But not all local authorities are equally generous or understanding to would-be dancers, which may lead to unfairness and loss of valuable talent.

This can sometimes be remedied by additional help from the Royal Ballet School's Endowment Fund, which can supplement the living allowance of exceptionally talented students. Even so in a particular year the standard of new recruits can fall through lack of local government support.

Obviously from an economic point of view the School must accept a certain number of students each year to balance its budget, which has been worked out far in advance and is based on the income it expects from fees. Therefore it can happen that 'borderline' applicants, who can afford to pay privately, must be accepted in lieu of more promising talents who cannot take up the positions offered them because the family income cannot adequately supplement their local authority grant.

In all fairness the parents of these students are advised of the frailty of their position and that their graduation into the Company is even less likely than for the more talented students. The fact remains though that hopes cannot but fail to be raised, and the resulting disillusionment can still be a traumatic experience.

It is far better to look the facts squarely in the face, and accept them early on, than be doubly disappointed later. You can still make use of the experience gained through this additional training, so long as you are aware of the possible termination of your chosen career, earlier than you had anticipated. You also have the opportunity to prepare and plan ahead during this time, for an alternative career (not necessarily outside the theatre.)

Every dancer has to consider this fact at some time or another during his or her career. For dancing, as a sole ambition, is such a very precarious choice to sustain. Apart from possible injuries, and accidents, a dancer's career is short at the best of times, and only a very few continue beyond their mid-thirties in an active capacity. So an alternative, whether it be an extension of dancing, such as character or mime roles, teaching or choreographing, or a complete contrast away from the theatre altogether, has always to be borne in mind. The sooner you are aware of this aspect of being a dancer the easier it is to make the transition when the time comes for it.

Footballers have the same problem and, if anything, their career life is even shorter than in ballet. One admires the foresight with which so many have planned for the future by laying the foundations of another business, while still involved in their first choice of profession. This is possibly a little harder for a dancer, whose time is usually more fully occupied, and whose work is really more demanding. I have known boys in the Company though who took courses in engineering and mathematics in preparation for a second career in the future.

It is a problem of greater consequence for boys than girls, usually anyway, and I have often wondered whether it is not perhaps some trick of fate, which invariably allows the boys in a company far more free time initially than the girls. Boys do not have any *corps de ballet* tradition, and therefore in many ways their actual chances of dancing in performances are even less than those of the girls.

It seems even more important then, that they should have some other interest or occupation to which they can turn during times of comparative freedom. Even if the opportunities to do anything constructive are limited, there is always the time to think and establish a few positive ideas which can be put into effect when necessary.

It is interesting that in the commercial theatre the exact reverse is true. Boys are in tremendous demand, and never seem to want for work. The opportunities for success are far greater, and very often considerably more rewarding both creatively and financially. At the same time, because the nature of the work is more spasmodic than that of the continuous season in a classical company, it is also easier to become involved in forming outside business enterprises. Girls on the other hand have an even greater struggle than classical dancers to achieve a foot-hold in the commercial theatre world, and there always seems to be a dozen or more girls for every job available.

I have rather strayed from my original point, and I should add here that being a fee-paying student is by no means synonymous with failure. Grants are not always available for everyone, and there is then no choice but to be a fee-paying student. There are of course scholarships which are also awarded to promising students, but these are few and far between. Many Commonwealth dancers have no alternative but to come as fee-paying students, and have later graduated into the Company, where we would be very much the poorer without them.

With time one hopes the situation may change so that all grants will be issued from the central Government and discrimination may be avoided. But it is always worthwhile to make enquiries about the current situation when you are auditioning.

Apart from this, rejection by the Royal Ballet should never be considered the last word on your career as a dancer. Your style and temperament may well be better suited to one of the many highly reputable companies abroad, or smaller companies here in England.

I started at the Royal Ballet School together with another 'Elmhurster' Geraldine Long, who later joined the Festival Ballet—in a very junior class. We both found this relegation very demoralising at the time, particularly as the third member of our trio, Diana, was separated from us and put in a more senior class. But we settled down, determined to work our way up. At least our training at Elmhurst had taught us the spirit of 'never say die'!

There was one extra class which I thoroughly enjoyed though, and this helped to maintain my spirits during this period. It was *pas de deux* work. Here at least was a chance for self-expression under the rumbustious direction and encouragement of Errol Addison. Caution was thrown to the winds, for he eradicated any fear of lifts and turns, and inspired the girls to have confidence in their partners. Two factors which are very necessary if you are going to enjoy *pas de deux* work, and make it an exciting but relaxed experience for the audience.

I had only one really rather unfortunate accident. Practising lifts with a boy after class, he lost his footing while I was balanced on my stomach in a 'Swallow' position on his shoulder. In order to save himself from falling he let go of me, with the result that I slid head first down his front to hit the floor with my chin!

I had to have three or four stitches in the cut, and did not have quite the same implicit trust in my partners for some time afterwards. Just to make matters worse, I was also used as an example to demonstrate to the rest of the School how dangerous it was to practise without supervision. I was completely mortified!

Gradually though things in general began to improve, and after the first two terms I was upgraded. As though miraculously all my original fears and depressions were dispelled as quickly as they had appeared. It took many years before I finally realised that the life of a dancer is rather like a perpetual switch-back railway. No sooner have you hit the bottom of a decline than you start to climb back up again, driven on by some hidden force.

The second year came round, and finally Diana, Geraldine and I were all together again. We were now in the 'graduates' class, which meant we did occasional work with the Company when 'extras' were needed. It was very exciting to be actually working with the Company, even though it added to the agony of wondering whether you would ever be a part of it.

We also did quite a lot of work with the Opera Ballet, and the first time I actually danced at Covent Garden was in *Aïda*. It was also my first encounter with the evils of 'wet-brown', a body make-up of thick brown liquid, diluted with water and applied with a sponge. It seemed to stay with you for days, no matter how hard you tried to scrub it off afterwards. It also had an embarrassing way of oozing out in brown rivulets when you began to sweat in class the next day, and it ruined your underwear. Nowadays, thankfully, pancake has practically replaced wet-brown although washing it off is still a fairly arduous task.

*Aïda* was an initiation into several of the perils of stage work not previously encountered. One of these was learning to ignore the twenty foot drop behind you, with only a frail safety net to prevent you falling while waiting to emerge from a cave-like tomb placed centre-stage. This, when you are shivering with nerves anyway, was no easy matter—especially when they forgot the safety net one night.

Another lesson was how to stand still, for what seemed like hours, in an Egyptian frieze, while a long aria was being sung by Radames. Much later, when I was in the Company, I learned this could be even worse, when you suddenly had to leap onto point after having stood rooted to the spot as a swan or wili, unable to move a muscle. I thought my ankles would break sometimes as I galoomphed around like a lumbering carthorse, trying to get the circulation moving again.

I continued to live at home, now Hampton Court, and travel up by Greenline bus each day. It was less expensive than living in a bed-sitter or sharing a flat in London. And as I was on a grant the money for living and travel expenses had to be eked out to the last half-penny. Many of my friends though, had the additional struggle of adapting to the problems of living on their own for the first time. Usually in flats shared with three or four friends.

In the long run this break from the security of home is probably best tackled while you are a student. Once you start working professionally, you already need to know how to stand on your own feet and be a reasonably self-reliant individual. Also if some of the practical problems of living and working alone have already been encountered, it makes the first few weeks in a company a far less overwhelming experience.

A flat shared with friends is obviously the most economical and least depressing answer to living accommodation. At least any emergencies or disasters can be met with a greater degree of equilibrium *en-masse*, than if you are alone. It always seems far more dramatic and ghastly if you have to cope on your own. A dancer's life is not easy at the best of times and there seems no point in adding to the discomforts by making your living conditions an added burden.

There are many newly discovered problems which also have an effect on your work. Boys suddenly find they have to learn how to sew, mend, darn, wash and cook for themselves, while girls are faced with fuse-boxes, electrical plugs, antique pilot lit fridges and gas water heaters, all of which demand a certain respect and understanding. Explosions, or worse, can happen unless you know how to handle them. I once had the bottom of an old, and very dirty water heater descend into the bath while I was still in it, the ensuing mess was appalling, and I emerged from the bath looking like an old-fashioned chimney sweep!

I feel it is important to mention a few of these mundane matters here, for all too often you are never warned about the difficulties and depressions of actually living alone. Your thoughts are understandably centred on the work and progress that must be made towards achieving a successful career, but the background conditions of how and where you live have just as great a bearing on your progress, because of the way in which they influence your attitude of mind.

I saw the work of many students dragged down because they were surrounded by problems of everyday life, which they had no idea how to control. It can be very upsetting after all, to wake up and find a small lake outside your bedroom window (because you have rented a cheap basement flat), and realise that you have got to wade through it in order to get to the outside lavatory—I know, it once happened when I was sharing a flat.

The strongest piece of advice I can offer is to recommend that you ask as many questions as you can think of, before you actually leave home, and try to learn from other friends how to avoid the most obvious pitfalls of flat-hunting and living. This should save you some of the more hair-raising experiences, although you are bound to encounter some . . . everyone does.

I suppose part of the reason why I place so much importance on this aspect of your life is because, in the dance world, outward appearances do matter. The way in which you conduct your personal life, as well as the way in which you present yourself for class, is observed by those who teach you, although you may be unaware of it. An assessment of your character is very often formed on the basis of this, and a resulting recommendation, or doubts as to your suitability for work in the theatre is handed on to potential employers. This applies as much to teachers who take open professional classes, as those who work within a school.

Anyone who engages you has only the impression gained from a brief audition to depend upon, they therefore try to work in close relationship with reputable teachers who have had longer to form a more rounded opinion. A classroom ensemble which is a grubby mass of holes and ladders can be taken as a sign of an undisciplined and careless nature, which could be reflected in performances.

This does not mean that it is necessary to go to the other extreme of regimented carefulness, but there is no doubt about it, clean and neat practice clothes are far less distracting and irritating to the eye, than an irregular conglomeration of assorted clothing. The hardest part of being a student is the fact that it is a period in your life when you are on trial both as an individual, and an artist.

While talking about these practical aspects of student life, I would like to mention again, the advisability of exploring further afield than the narrow confines of the dancing world, for now is the time to do it. It is worth remembering that what might merely be an awakening and awareness to new interests and hobbies now, could be the means of earning a livelihood in the future.

Accidents, illness and injury are all to much a part of a dancer's life, as I saw and eventually discovered for myself. A curiosity in your attitude towards the world and other people, helps to soften the blow should your career as a dancer be abruptly terminated. For you will already be aware that there are other things in life, apart from dancing. I would not be writing this book now if I had not realised there were an awful lot of other things I really wanted to do, as well as dancing.

The other thing about following up outside interests while you are a student, is that it prevents boredom and loneliness. These can take over very easily when you are left with time on your hands between classes, and also in the evenings when you are no longer a part of the familiar family routine and pattern. Even though you may be living with friends, they have their own lives to lead too, and you are often left to your own devices. Books from libraries, Art Galleries, cheap seats at concerts on the South Bank or gallery seats at the theatre, are all inexpensive ways of stimulating the imagination and opening up new areas of discovery and exploration. It is also occasionally a way of making new friends.

Less obvious, but equally interesting are the fine examples of craftsmanship on show at the sale rooms of Sotheby's and Christie's, a fascinating way of discovering an interest in silver, antiques or porcelain, which perhaps you never guessed you possessed. On a more practical, but really equally eloquent and creative level, a knowledge and interest in food and wine can be more than a way of keeping body and soul together. Although as a student you are of course somewhat restricted by your purse, your diet is important, so you might as well make it interesting as well as nourishing!

I realise you may feel I have strayed rather from the point of 'life as a dancer', but believe me, in many ways this is as much a part of what eventually comes over in performance, as is the technical skill achieved through the actual work in the classroom.

But to continue, I auditioned successfully into the Company before the end of the second year. It was a hair-raising experience of elimination through four classes, which contained progressively fewer and fewer candidates. Eventually eight of us were accepted out of the original one hundred and fifty possibles and, with a certain degree of relief, we were able to give our full attention to the present work in hand.

The pace of work had increased considerably during the second year, for apart from the School's end-of-year performance, presented by the students in a matinee at Covent Garden, we were also involved in more and more of the Company performances.

The School's performance was a great opportunity to tackle some of the classical roles actually in repertory. Words failed me when I was told I would be dancing the Prelude in *Les Sylphides*, for it is one of the most romantic and ethereal pieces I could ever have hoped to dance. My romantic dreams and ideals had at least in part, been realised. Equally wonderful was the fact that a new ballet was created for us by Kenneth Macmillan— *Suite Provençale* to music of the same name by Poulenc.

It was a marvellous experience and opportunity for students to work so closely with such a well-established choreographer. As with most choreographers, he had the ability to induce us to achieve things we would otherwise have considered impossible, and we determined to prove that his hopes would not be disappointed. A fine example of just what is possible when mind triumphs over matter!

I believe the ballet itself was not considered to be one of Kenneth's better works but we thought it was marvellous, and gave it all our worth. Certainly he gained eight devotees, as new recruits to the Company.

At the same time we were learning another of his ballets in the repertoire, *Baiser de la Fée*. It had a smallish *corps de ballet* and, because of a sudden spate of sickness and injury in the Company Diana and I found ourselves thrown on one night with only a few hours warning. Ironically our first entrance, which was in pairs, meant that Diana and I were together. We knew it followed a blackout, and a cloth would go up in front of us as the lights came up, but we were none too sure when it all happened. Nervously trotting up and down in the wings we were just about to ask one of the boys, when he grabbed us hastily out of the way of a rapidly descending piece of scenery, and shoved us behind it.

In a flash the lights were up, the entrance music playing and we were on. The shock of seeing the audience when we least expected it, shot us into action, and mercifully we ended up where we were supposed to start the dance.

At about the same time a number of us were very honoured to receive a personal letter from Dame Margot Fonteyn, requesting our participation in the annual charity Gala for the Royal Academy of Dancing at Drury Lane. She was to dance Act II *Swan Lake* partnered by Nureyev, with Yehudi Menuhin playing the violin solo for their *pas de deux*. We were to provide part of the *corps de ballet*, together with some of the Company members.

As you can imagine no-one refused such a marvellous opportunity. As it happened Michael Soames had to replace an indisposed Nureyev for the performance, but I do not think we will ever be likely to hear such a moving rendering of that piece of music. Certainly, I have never again felt so exhilerated, to the degree that I was totally unconscious of the usual agony of standing fossilised during its performance.

Events had followed so fast on top of one another in those last few weeks that eventually we developed a certain numbness to any new demands. There were certainly no complaints of lack of work—rather the opposite. I also began to understand the effect and concern one's work can cause to others as well as one-self at such critical times.

My mother was quietly suffering agonies trying to suppress her concern at my increasing thinness, and socket-like eyes. She had learned however that it would be meaningless to say anything at this point, as I was too wrapped up in the progress of events for it to make any difference. A selfish attitude admittedly, but one unfortunately demanded by ballet, if you are to succeed at such times. It helps to learn how to handle these demands with both tact and diplomacy as you get older though, for boyfriends or husbands are understandably less happy about accepting these conditions!

We had one more unique experience before our graduate year finally ended. It was the year that the new Coventry Cathedral

was consecrated and there was a special service for, and from the
Arts. Dame Ninette de Valois was asked to create a masque, for
which she chose to depict Terpsichore and her eight muses.
This was performed barefoot in the Sanctuary, in itself an inno-
vation for it must be a very long time since a Church Sanctuary
has been used for dancing.

I was thrilled when Dame Ninette chose me to dance Terpsichore, and it was through working with her on this solo that my
admiration and affection for her developed. I have a great deal
to thank her for, not least my acceptance into the Company,
which fortunately for me she was determined on despite my big
drawback—thinness. Strange as it may sound, it is worth remembering that it is as bad to be too thin as too fat on stage. As one
critic aptly put it 'it lent my work a certain coltish quality'. I was
more like an animated pin-man on occasions than a supposedly
fully-fledged swan!

But to return to the masque just briefly, one strange coincidence
was, that included in the programme of speakers and singers was
my former idol, Christopher Hassall. After all these years I was
performing and conversing with a man I had revered as a child.
It became a very special occasion for me because of this.

Through our work, we had developed a common bond, that
made me begin to realise the quality of the theatre's immense
and all-embracing family atmosphere. It provides a security which
people in the theatre so desperately need, and which they are so
often without in their individual lives, away from the theatre.
Its members are always ready to support, encourage, or boost
morale whenever it is needed, with a sincerity not always associated with the theatre.

# 5

## ON TOUR WITH THE ROYAL BALLET

STARTING WORK WITH THE COMPANY was almost exactly like the initial year in the School, with all the same disappointments and disillusionments. This time though it began to dawn on me at last that ballet is composed of not one but several ladders. Consequently it means dropping back several rungs each time you reach the top of one ladder, in order to start climbing the next one. Once you have become reconciled to this fact, the effect is not quite so depressing.

The first six months seemed very barren, with almost less performance than when I had been a graduate. There was plenty to learn though, in the way of repertoire, and in retrospect I was glad I had those six months to observe and digest some of the policy, structure and hierarchy of Company life. It was all very bewildering at first, despite our preview as graduates. At the time of course, we did not realise that once we were accepted into the Company, we constituted a threat to the position of the older *coryphées* within the Company.

Whenever new members are accepted there is always an element of unrest, as everyone secretly wonders whether this is the 'beginning of the end' for them. In actual fact there were very few who really made life uncomfortable; the majority were extremely helpful and kind, passing on invaluable tips about hair-styles, make-up, etc; as well as hauling us through the terrifying *corps de ballet* rehearsals.

This I learned later was in fact to their own advantage anyway, as the more help they gave us towards learning the steps and formations, the faster the rehearsal of something they had done

umpteen times before, was over! But it quickly taught us the
use of diplomacy on all fronts, and discretion at all times. A few
newcomers are fairly tough-skinned and seem totally insensitive
to any ill-feeling, but I found it easier if you acknowledged your
inferiority, and acted accordingly.

Although I did not realise it, a very big change in my life with
the Company was to occur at the end of the first six months. The
Company was composed of two halves, one Touring and one
Resident section. In actual fact both did a little of each, but their
names denoted the more prominent proportion. There was a
time when they were known as the 'First' and 'Second' Companies,
but this had unfortunate connotations with first and second class.
A point hotly disputed and eventually proved more than ill-
founded. However it was decided that six of us were to go on an
exchange scheme, whereby six of the Touring members became
Resident, while we gained the experience of life in the Touring
Company. And it certainly was an experience.

I shall never forget that first tour. It was a miracle it did not put
me off ballet, touring and the theatre for good. We joined in the
January of one of the coldest winters for years. Snow had already
fallen and at the first place we went to, Southend-on-Sea, the
sea was frozen all along the shoreline. We seemed to encounter
more hazards during those fourteen weeks than on any subsequent
tour.

This was probably because it was so new to us, for it was not
only the physical hardships that seemed so numerous, there were all
the agonies and ignominies of being an inexperienced underling,
with no real knowledge of what stage craft was all about. Suddenly all that we had learned at Elmhurst seemed infinitesimal
in comparison to what we were now learning.

Finally there was the grim introduction to the joys of travelling
up and down England by British Rail on Sundays, and discovering
the unknown quantity and quality of each town's digs. Yet
somehow it all added up to one of the most enthralling and
exciting periods in my life, and strangely enough convinced me
that this was the sort of life I wanted.

The horror stories of touring are never-ending and, in retrospect, provide ample material for cheering ourselves when in the midst of even more depressing circumstances. The dressing room would resound to the gales of laughter as we recalled past disasters, and tears of mirth rolled down our faces, ruining any attempts to apply eye-lines or mascara. It was better than tears of genuine distress though, which had to be avoided at all costs; their infectious laughter could have disastrous results by devastating not just the make-up but morale as well.

It would take far too long to tell the whole saga of that tour, but it is worthwhile recounting some of the experiences since they are typical of life with a touring company, and things that happened on the tours which followed. The knowledge gained in the techniques of stage presence, and general theatre craft are also typical of what every newcomer to a company must expect to go through.

Once again you are on trial, but now your career depends entirely on your powers of survival both mental and physical. You seem to be tried in every direction at once, until you feel like giving up because everything you do seems to be the wrong thing at the wrong time. I mentioned earlier the hierarchy of a company, a system which exists even in the most democratic of companies, and which in many ways is comparable to submitting to the bureaucracy of school prefects.

There is no form of retaliation, or even the chance of defending your own rights if you intend to live a fairly happy co-existence with the rest of the Company; merely an acceptance of your limited experience in comparison with everyone else. I tried to stand up for my rights once, and was eventually reduced to tears half of rage, half mortification.

It was also a lesson in the importance of pride in the manner in which you present yourself on stage. We had to keep our *pointe* shoes in good condition for performances, checking that the ribbons blended with our flesh-coloured tights, which also must not be too light or dark a pink.

We cleaned our shoes with methylated or surgical spirits,

then powdered them with talcum powder to dull the sheen of
the satin, which again is unattractively heightened under a blue
light. This is very effective initially but after a while the dirty
patches tend to spread into the shoe in a pale grey mass. We had
a quota of shoes issued each week but, doing eight performances
a week, it was very difficult to keep them clean, and to prevent
them wearing through before the next issue was due. This was
particularly so when some of the stages were really filthy, and
caked with hard black oily flakes which stuck to the satin like
glue.

After one performance of *Swan Lake* we were panting upstairs
to the dressing-room, when one of the more senior *coryphées*
called after me and told me to look at my shoes. I have always
felt it was taking unfair advantage as we had just been kneeling
all over the stage—but anyway, I stopped and looked and apart
from a couple of very recent smudges I could not see anything
wrong.

However for the sake of an example, I was thoroughly up-
braided in front of the rest of the Company, for appearing in
such an unprofessional manner. I tried to tell her I had cleaned
them just before going on stage, but was immediately repri-
manded, in face of the facts, for impudence! Utterly defeated,
I stood and listened, with everyone else, to a total condemnation
of my irresponsible attitude, which hurt my sense of professional
pride more than anything.

It did bring home to me though how super careful one has to
be in matters of appearance. Nothing can be out of place, not a
hair or shoe ribbon-end must be exposed, and later on, with
each successive year I saw new recruits making exactly the same
mistakes. It was always up to the older Company members to
correct them and put them on the right path, although I hasten
to add, with a little more tact than the manner in which I had been
dealt with, on that occasion.

In a sense it was an understandable reaction, for one takes an
immense pride in the Company, and in particular the performances
which you, as a part of it, present. It is maddening when you see

someone with an apparently slovenly approach who has marred the whole effect, and ruined everything you are trying to achieve. There is no doubt about it: one figure out of place or out of character, is more obvious than all the other carefully groomed portrayals by everyone else.

Placing and positioning are another lesson which can never be learned until you are actually working in a *corps de ballet*. It takes a full year to become a reasonably good member of a *corps de ballet*, but it is one of the best disciplines and trainings for knowing how to use the stage space available, and learning consideration for your fellow members.

Boys obviously do not have to endure this form of regimentation, and consequently have far greater difficulty in keeping together and on place, when they do have to work together in a group. One example of what can happen as a result, was the day I received a hearty punch on the jaw from my partner who, in an excess of enthusiasm, had failed to take account of the amount of stage space available to the pair of us in relation to everyone else. I think it was the first time I really knew what was meant by 'seeing stars'.

Personally I consider this period in the *corps de ballet* as being one of the most challenging aspects of being in a company, and I always found it extremely hard to conform to the necessary requirements.

I had never realised before how awful the conditions were, and still are in some of the provincial towns, and how cramped such a big Company can be backstage—let alone on stage. I often used to wonder on Monday mornings, when we first arrived at the theatre, how on earth we would ever perform in such a small area. At times it really was quite ridiculous.

Perhaps the smallest theatre we performed in was the Arts Theatre, Cambridge. A beautiful little theatre but quite inadequate for the size of our Company. Even the central Green-room, off which all the dressing-rooms opened, was converted into the Wardrobe's domain. Modesty in any degree was virtually impossible, as there simply was not room for us all to change costumes within the confines of the dressing-rooms, and a relay system would have wasted valuable time in the intervals.

So there was nothing for it but to grab a dressing-gown, shed your costume in the nearest available space, and then retreat to the dressing-room. Nobody seemed to worry unduly though, and one realised the extent to which a touring Company very quickly became a rather oversized family.

The stage presented more trying problems however, and I came to dread return visits to the theatre, knowing the sort of performance one would be forced to present. *Swan Lake* Act II was reduced to six swans a side for the *corps de ballet*, and even then the back few girls, of which I was one, being fairly tall—got tied up with the netting on the backcloth; while those at the front were in danger of landing up in the laps of the first row of the audience. They would have missed the orchestra pit all together, for one could almost shake hands with the audience over its narrow width.

I will never forget, after I had been with the Company for some years, doing Queen of the Wilis, in Act II *Giselle* in Cambridge; I was supposed to make a dramatic entrance twice in the ballet in a series of *jêtés* travelling downstage. In order to fit it all in though I was forced to do one *jêté* forward and two steps back, which must have looked quite ludicrous.

It became very depressing having to perform under these circumstances and it could even be quite dangerous. One boy smashed his foot on a heavy stage weight, when making a speedy exit. This resulted in a very nasty bruise and cracked toe joint. We also felt angry at not being able to give of our best, to such devoted and enthusiastic audiences. The people of Cambridge were staunch supporters and they, together with the delightful environment of the town itself were the things that made a week there bearable.

We did not always play the theatres though. All too often converted cinemas were used, and these were totally devoid of any atmosphere at all. Someone once aptly described such an auditorium, built like an underground tunnel, as being similar to playing to audiences in an aeroplane hangar. The audience seemed to stretch into infinity, with no balcony, or dress-circle to break up the monotonous depth. There was also the problem of the children's Saturday morning film show, which still had to be projected. This meant the screen had to be lowered in front of the stage, making any access to it quite impossible before the performance.

I particularly remember the incongruity of coming in for the matinee of *Sleeping Beauty* at Ipswich and stumbling through a darkened auditorium of screaming children watching a Wild West shooting match. It somehow destroyed any shred of magic one might hope to conjure up for the afternoon. At Ipswich, because of the usual lack of changing space upstairs, the wide panniered court costumes were kept under the stage amongst the Company's travelling skips. What we did not realise though, until a small boy in the stalls made it patently obvious, was that the door which led onto the orchestra pit failed to fasten properly and gave the audience a grandstand view of half the *corps de ballet*, clad in tights and bras, attempting to clamber into their cumbersome costumes.

Ipswich had a lot to answer for as far as I and several others were concerned on that first tour. The snow was already two feet deep and frozen hard, with a north-easterly wind blowing down from Russia, or so it seemed. Apart from the major problem of the cinema itself, the changing-rooms, far from being too cold were ironically stifling hot, being situated next to the boiler room, which gave off the most terrible carbon monoxide fumes. Consequently, they made us feel half-doped most of the time, so that we were forced to trudge around the town in the freezing cold in order to keep awake.

Finding accommodation for a company as big as ours proved difficult in the small towns, and once again Ipswich was no exception. I used to share digs with Patricia Ruanne (who later became a principal of the Royal Ballet and is now a ballerina with the Festival Ballet) and we were comparatively well off on this occasion compared to some of the others. At least the landlord was friendly, even if the room was incredibly spartan and break-fast consisted of our boiling water in mugs, brought from the theatre, by means of an antiquated heating element, and provid-ing our own coffee.

But three of our *corps de ballet* friends, plumping for a reasonably cheap choice of lodgings, ran into rather unusual difficulties, and had to leave post-haste when they discovered over Sunday tea, that their landlady was still an avid Nazi supporter, and was determined to spend the week plying them with all manner of literature in the hopes of winning them over to 'The Cause'!

Ipswich had one final parting shot for us though. A group of us decided to drive back to London on the Saturday night after the last show, in a Bedford van owned by one of the boys. It started to snow as we left the town, and by the time we were out on the Essex flats a blinding storm was well under way—and there, the Bedford breathed its last. No amount of pushing, shoving or 'waiting for the engine to cool' could coax it into life; so there we sat rapidly disappearing into a snow-drift.

It was not to be our final hour however, as we were rescued, and brought back to London crammed into the back of a Pop Group's equally ancient van. Thankfully theirs made it all the way to London, where we eventually fell out at Marble Arch at four o'clock in the morning.

Another stop on our itinerary, Derby, provided a rather trying occasion, when another friend and I had to share a double bed. It was in fact our landlady's bed which she nobly relinquished for a divan bed at the foot of it, and I regret to add she was a heavy snorer! I do not think we had a decent night's sleep all week, for we were so afraid of disturbing one another that I would wake with my face plastered against the wall on one side, while Sandy was literally hanging over the edge on the other side.

Meanwhile our dear landlady, who was typically Northern in her generous-heartedness, had her house packed with homeless dancers. One boy was on a put-u-up divan in the sitting room while one of the musicians from the orchestra slept on a mattress on the floor, and Pat was in a sort of box-room sleeping on a cast iron ottoman which was a little shorter than she was!

It was in Derby also I remember that the dressing-rooms were so tiny that the five chairs became jammed together. If one person got in or out we all did. This became rather tiresome, so eventually we developed a certain athletic ability for leaping over the backs of the chairs. Once we were all in though we discovered that the door stuck behind the last chair and could never be shut. That was a week of continuous laughter which sometimes came very close to tears.

But these incidents are enough to give you a fair idea of the hilarious sort of life you can expect on tour; however hollow the laughter may be sometimes.

At the end of the tour, we were supposed to return to the Resident section. They were preparing for a three month tour of America, and as the *corps de ballet* had to kept to a minimum, Pat and I were told that, as we were the youngest, we would have to be left behind. Instead we would stay with the Touring section for their Season in London at the Opera House.

That decided it, we both independently came to the same conclusion that we wanted to stay for good. It had an atmosphere in which we were both very happy, and by now we had made some good friends among the rest of the Company. So what had started as a temporary arrangement, which we had approached with great foreboding and trepidation, now turned out to be the real answer to our future progress in the Company. Naturally we were sorry not to be going to America, but by staying with the Touring section our chances of travel in the future were just as great.

Once again we had the opportunity of working with Kenneth Macmillan during the London Season, on a revival which almost amounted to a completely new interpretation of *House of Birds*. To my immense surprise, apart from being chosen, together with Pat as one of the small group of eight bird/friends, I was to understudy the role of the Birdwoman herself. Although I knew it would take a miracle for me actually to perform it, at least I had the chance to rehearse it, which at that point was almost as exciting.

While we had been on tour, we had been performing *Checkmate*, the ballet by Dame Ninette de Valois with music specially composed by Sir Arthur Bliss. It was always an exciting ballet to do, and now back in London we were to film it for television. Beryl Grey danced the role of the Black Queen which was originally created for her, and similarly Sir Robert Helpman played the role of the old Red King, who is lured into her trap. Dame Ninette herself directed proceedings, with Margaret Dale producing.

I had never realised before how time-consuming a business filming is, with every camera angle having to be mapped out and recorded. This involved an endless amount of standing around or holding positions while little bits of coloured sticky tape were stuck on the floor to mark the exact spot you had to reach at a given moment in every run through. In the end there were so many different coloured strips, we could none of us remember which was which, and what they were supposed to indicate.

It took a week of solid rehearsing before we finally spent the entire day and most of the evening shooting it at the B.B.C. studios. It was something of a shock to discover that as Black Pawns we had to have grey make-up for our faces, in order to show the contrast against the Red Pawns, on a black and white film. The Red Pawns had an even worse fate though, as their normally red costumes were now yellow, again for reasons of contrast.

Unfortunately the dye was absorbed into their skins under the blazing lights of the studio, and they left the studios that night looking like a tribe of jaundiced pygmies.

The whole Season was hard work, mounting new ballets and revivals and, coming at the end of nearly a year of touring and working under bad conditions, the strain for the rest of the Company was especially hard. It was imperative that the Company should make a good showing in comparison with the recently departed Resident section, for I am afraid competition between the two Companies was extremely fierce. The reception we had from both the audiences and the critics was more than favourable though, and our efforts were well rewarded.

Oddly enough although the studios at Barons Court were a joy to work in, there were many days when conditions seemed no better than when we were on tour. This happened when we had morning calls on stage at the Royal Opera House at Covent Garden, and there was only time for a *barre* by way of a warm-up beforehand. As the studio in the Opera House is minute, it meant either a relay system of two or three consecutive *barres,* or struggling on the carpet in the Crush Bar upstairs!

The still constant cry for expansion at the Opera House will hopefully be resolved with the G.L.C.'s scheme for the whole of Covent Garden, but in the meantime life continues as before.

The trials and tribulations of that year had been many, but I knew by the end that the whole of the first year in a Company is really no more than a paid apprenticeship in studying the subtleties and finer points of your art. I was also to learn some years later that a seemingly uneventful stage fall (a not uncommon occurrence on the badly surfaced provincial stages) was to prove literally that in my beginning lay my end!

Elmhurst may not have prepared me for some of the disasters but thankfully it had taught me quite a bit about stagecraft and presence of mind needed in an emergency. This saved me from some of the additional harassments which beset a few of my friends.

Such things as realising that you do not hang onto stage lights and scenery, in order to warm up in the wings, because it weakens the structure. This once happened in *Les Patineurs* when all the trellised arches folded, one after the other like a pack of cards. Then knowing what upstage, downstage, prompt and O.P. mean for directional moves, even when the fear of doing the wrong thing can make you panic to the point of forgetting the difference between your left and right foot; learning to move in costumes that are heavy and courtly, hamper every gesture, both yours and your partner's and can have an embarrassing way of bringing you to your knees when walking upstairs because you have walked up the inside of the skirt.

Really if you can survive that first year, you can survive virtually anything.

# 6

## THE GROWTH OF A REPERTOIRE

PAT AND I HAD APPROACHED John Field, the Director of the Touring Group, just before the end of the season, and asked if he would be prepared to keep us on with the Touring Company for the next year. He agreed, and started to make the necessary arrangements. Fate decided otherwise as far as I was concerned though, for a steadily rumbling appendix reached the point where its continued presence was intolerable. Consequently, after a brief holiday abroad, where it continued to grumble ominously, I returned hastily home for its removal.

Although I made a very quick recovery, Dame Ninette insisted that the rigours of touring would be too great, and I must stay with the Resident section. There was nothing I could do but accept the inevitable, and hope my return to the Touring Company would not be too long delayed.

I knew it would not be easy back with the Resident section for several reasons. Competition is bound to exist between two managements, even within the same Company. The manager of each section is responsible for the success or failure of his part of the Company and its productions. He is therefore anxious to keep a unification of spirit by retaining the same dancers for a period of time. In this way he can establish a sound and well co-ordinated *corps de ballet*, as well as having the chance to coach and produce Soloists and Principals in productions with which they are familiar.

A dancer who joins a company as a guest-artist, needs to be both experienced and composed in order to adapt to the subtleties and variations of individual productions. In a lesser degree the

same applies to a member of the *corps de ballet*. It is disturbing
for the *corps* to have constant changes amongst its ranks, and it
can often create irregularities in performance. It is understandable
therefore, that the manager of the Resident section should have
been reluctant to have me in the Company on a temporary
basis.

A wholehearted belief in your Company and its manager,
is very important if you are to establish any feeling of good-will.
As far as I was concerned, although I was still overjoyed at the
prospect of working with the Royal Ballet, I merely wished to
work in an environment to which I knew I was more suited.
Unfortunately it just so happened I fitted in better with the
Touring than the Resident section.

It was not an easy situation, especially as I was now unfamiliar
with some of the repertoire acquired during the American tour.
The result was that I was cast for very few actual performances.
This was understandable, and in the light of more recent experience, when I have been in the position to help form cast lists,
I can appreciate the reluctance to cast someone in a part which
they are ultimately going to relinquish, for this means re-rehearsal
for their replacement after a few months. It is far easier to cast
someone who is on a more permanent basis, and leave the drifter
as cover (i.e. understudy). I felt completely rejected at the time
however, and consequently a terrible failure.

All clouds have their silver linings though if you look hard
enough, and this period with the Company was to serve me well
in later years. I developed an ability for quick-wittedness, learning
everyone's place in the *corps de ballet*, and thereby gaining a
reputation for being able to step in at a moment's notice, without
undue rehearsal, and yet with complete reliability. It was self-
preservation really, for in this way I was almost able to guarantee
my being used whenever a cover was needed as replacement in a
performance. So there were a few bonuses to be gained even at
that point.

This ability to pick up steps is something which some people
find much easier than others. It depends on whether you have a

capacity for retaining or memorising visual patterns and shapes. I was very fortunate in that I have a photographic memory, and can literally store away in my mind 'rolls of film' as it were, recording what I have seen, and want to remember in detail. I can then unroll that particular 'film' whenever it is required.

For instance, the only way I can find my way around in a town, or in the country, is by memorising all the streets or fields and their inter-relation with one another, as I have no sense of direction at all, and have to rely on my 'photographic' images. Years later on returning to the same place, providing there have been no drastic changes, I can find my way around fairly accurately, with the help of my mental street-plan. In the same way I find it possible to memorise all the formations and patterns as well as the steps in ballets, so that I can see the whole effect in my mind as I put the results into practice.

When I first joined the Company, I was put on very hastily in *Rites of Spring* because somebody fell sick. It is not an easy ballet to learn, and the music then was very tricky to count because of the ever-changing bar lengths to which we were still unaccustomed. However, the fact that I had seen the dress rehearsal as a student some eighteen months earlier, held me in good stead.

The ballet had made a tremendous impression on me and so I had 'stored away' a fair amount of its overall shape. This, together with the detail I had just begun to learn in rehearsal, meant that I was able to go on with only a run-through on stage, without music, before the performance, and manage to get through the performance without any major mistakes.

But as I say, not everyone's mind works in this way, and I was just very fortunate to be able to use this particular asset. For many people it remains a hard slog of constant repetition, until the steps are firmly embedded in their memories.

I did have one brief respite from just being a cover however, when the Touring section went to Paris for a Festival week at the *Theatre de Champs Elysées*. There were several people off sick, and I was sent for as a replacement. I was thrilled and played down my still recent recovery from appendicitis in order that I should go. The Resident section gave their consent, as I was not needed for performances at the Opera House during that time.

It was a wonderful week as well as being my first taste of the delightful difference between touring abroad and in England. There was an air of excitement all the time and, although we had to work hard giving six performances of *Swan Lake* in five days, the pleasures of Paris were not passed by. There were several receptions we had to attend given by the Embassies, the Theatre, and the *Hotel de Ville,* which to me were a novelty and a chance to see inside places one would never normally be allowed to enter.

Somehow we managed to survive on very little sleep, and my appendix scar held out  Although I do remember collapsing in a breathless heap flat on my back on the concrete floor of the dressing-room at the end of Act II—hardly able to struggle into my Mazurka boots in time for Act III—yet begging my friends not to tell the ballet mistress for fear I would be sent home!

All too soon I had to say goodbye to the Company and return to London, sadly knowing I would miss yet another tour abroad later that year when the Touring section went to Baalbek.

It was a fairly full year at Covent Garden for new productions and, as I was only partially involved in these, I had time fully to observe the success or failure of various choreographic and production techniques. It was information I could store away for future use. And indeed, later on I did find it unexpectedly very valuable.

It might be helpful at this point to discuss a little more fully, exactly what is involved in choreographing and producing a new ballet, or mounting a revival. The first day of rehearsal of a new ballet is always a fairly tense time. The choreographer finally has to substantiate the ideas he has been mentally formulating over the previous weeks, while the dancers are equally nervous wondering whether they will be able to realise these dreams. If no new works or revivals have been produced for a fairly long time there is the additional effort of making the brain function at a much faster level of assimilation than usual.

It is rather like riding a bicycle; once you have learned how to ride the memory never leaves you, but there is a certain knack and aptitude which, unless it is kept in constant use, becomes a little rusty with time, and it needs a few trial runs before you are roadworthy again. So it is with the ability to pick up steps and combinations set by a choreographer. Some are half-formed requiring a solution through the practical movements of the dancers, while others are totally formed, but tricky and complex to learn and perform.

After the first two or three days though, everyone settles down to a traditional pattern of rehearsals, and the pace of work usually picks up considerably. Even so there are always the days when nothing constructive seems to materialise, and every idea leads to a dead end. Very often anything that is decided upon may well be scrapped the next day in the light of fresh inspiration.

This perhaps is only to be expected, for the degree of creativity involved in any art is bound to fluctuate with the moods and emotions of those involved. A sculptor will find his material, whether it is stone, wood or clay as unresponsive and unsympathetic on some days, as will the choreographer find the dancers unwieldy and uninspiring. The two have to work in sympathy in order to produce a satisfactory end result.

Rehearsals are only a part of any production. For there are costume and wig-fittings to be arranged and the choreographer is, of course, in constant consultation with the designer to ensure that his choreographic schemes work within the context of the set, and that the costumes will not prove too great a hindrance to the individual and combined movements of the dancers.

Sometimes certain props are brought to the studio rehearsals so that the dancers can become accustomed to working with them, or parts of a costume are worn to see what difficulties may be encountered. In this way some of the problems of working in a costume can be overcome before reaching the stage rehearsals, for by then the steps have become too much an integral part of the ballet for the choreographer to want to consider changing them.

One particular instance of this was in *House of Birds* (music by

Mompou) where we had to wear a framework of wings attached
to a harness and in all measuring about three to four feet across.
In addition to this difficult and cumbersome apparatus, we also
wore feathered domino masks, over which an entire wicker
bird-cage enclosed the head completely, held in place yet
again with a complicated harness. As a finishing touch the
cage-door, placed directly in front of the face had to be opened
at a certain point in the ballet, and the safety catch on this had a
nasty habit of breaking loose so that the cage door flapped to
and fro as you danced.

I well remember seeing the agonised facial expressions from
behind the bars, as somebody's cage-door swung open, for no
amount of surreptitious adjustments with the angle of the head
would get it to close. As you can imagine we started to work
with these accoutrements as soon as they were made, for the
entire weight of the outfit pulled you wildly off balance initially.

There were problems with the feathers on the mask too. These
caught in the bars of the cage and locked your head in a permanent
and inextricable position. Happening constantly this really must
have given us a good approximation to a lot of twittering caged
birds, for there was a continuous flurry of battering feathers
against the bars, as one or other of us would attempt to free the
ensnared mask.

The noise of beating wings was in fact an integral part of the
ballet for, with our hands held against our rib-cages, we had to
beat the feathered wings with our elbows. Another painful
business which resulted in many bruised and battle-scarred elbow
bones. Our final hassle with this ensemble came near the end of
the ballet when we had an incredibly quick change out of the
entire costume, and into our transformation dresses and head-
dresses as young village girls and boys.

The first dress rehearsal was a disaster on this account, for even
with the marvellous and unruffled help of our dressers, we arrived
on stage thoroughly dishevelled. Some were still half-dressed,
and the total effect was as if we had recently spent the night in a
hay-stack, instead of being freshly released from the spell that

61

1 Class continues with the stage as classroom while on tour

WORK IN PROGRESS

2 A welcome pause while others rehearse

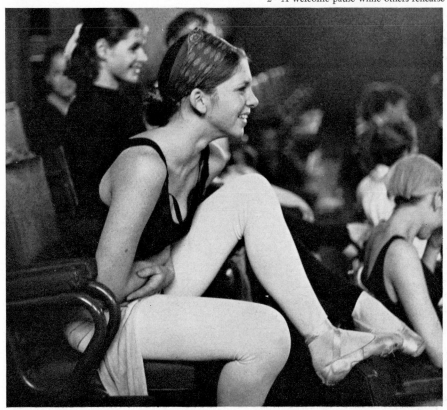

3 Dance as an important
   factor in television and
   stage revues

4 William Louther's vitality
   and dynamism in the
   'Graham' style. *Conso-
   lation of the Rising Moon*—
   Contemporary Dance
   Company

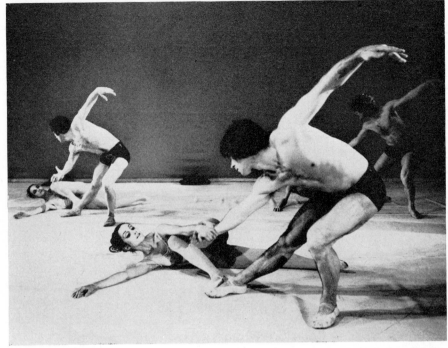

5  Modern dance married to the classical music of Beethoven. *Grosse Fuge*—Royal Ballet New Group

MODERN AND CONTEMPORARY DANCE

6  *Stages*—Contemporary Dance Company. An athletic concept choreographed by the Company's Director, Bob Cohan

7   Dame Margot Fonteyn and Rudolf Nureyev with the *Corps de Ballet* in Petipa style: *La Bayadère*
—Royal Ballet

IN THE CLASSIC TRADITION

8   *The Flower Festival: pas de deux*—Royal Ballet. The author with Paul Clarke in this Bournonville
extract

9   The ecstasy of dance in action. *Septet Extra*—Royal Ballet New Group

DESIGN IN MOVEMENT

10   Classical precision graced with style. *La Bayadère*—Royal Ballet

11 'The Wardrobe' (seated on the inevitable skip) both a vital part of any Company

PREPARATIONS FOR PERFORMANCE

12 An idyllic environment, as the author takes the Royal Ballet for class on an open-air stage abroad

13 Kenneth MacMillan choreo-
graphs *The Poltroon* for the
Royal Ballet New Group

14 After the dress rehearsal for a
Covent Garden production of
*The Dream*, the director's secretary distributes his notes to the
cast

FINALE: CURTAIN CALL

15   Dame Margot Fonteyn and Rudolf Nureyev receive the appreciation of their audience

had held us as captive birds. We didn't feel as though the magic had been an unqualified success either!

Another vivid memory and the first of many occasions, was the premiere of a new ballet on tour. *Summer's Night* by Peter Wright was premiered at Stratford-upon-Avon. It was chiefly memorable for the early morning stage-calls. They began at nine o'clock and seemed to follow hard on the heels of the previous night's performance. We seemed to be working all day and night, until there came a point when we wondered whether it was worthwhile leaving the theatre at all to go to bed.

It was a time of increasing desperation and frustration too, for we were so drunk with tiredness in the mornings that we literally reeled about on the stage. The illusion of being drunk was added to by having a gauze front cloth between us and the audience which, from the stage, gives the auditorium a glazed and blurry appearance. As a result of this 'drunkenness', we merely added to the number of prolonged and agonised hours needed to work on, and clean up the ballet for the first night.

We were almost too numb by the time the first night arrived to feel nervous or excited at all. But as the overture began, so did the familiar prickling sensation of half-thrill, half-fear which somehow brings that added strength and sparkle to a performance.

These dress rehearsals are in fact the next stage in a production, once the ballets are choreographically complete, and the first night date begins to loom ominously near. It is at this point that more often than not, an atmosphere of utter gloom descends over everyone concerned, and there is that ghastly feeling that the whole thing is doomed to failure.

The choreographer doubts whether he has achieved what he set out to do, the dancers fear everything will collapse because they cannot dance it, the music suddenly sounds completely different in orchestration, as opposed to the rehearsal piano or pre-recorded tapes, and the costumes and sets seem to provide insurmountable difficulties.

Gradually though as the shock of actually putting the whole thing on stage wears off, cuts and alterations can be made constructively to overcome unforeseen problems of working in the set. You begin to find phrases and certain instrumental sections in the orchestra which you realise carry the theme more strongly than the piano alone, and so everyone works towards pulling the pieces together to shape the ballet into something which has a totality and soundness.

In actual fact the orchestra are not called in until three or four days before the first night for a one-act ballet, as the cost for rehearsing musicians is prohibitive and has to be kept to a minimum. Not a moment can be wasted of the precious time with them—so nobody stops for breath—until they do!

Costumes however carefully designed and fitted beforehand, invariably provide some additional difficulties during rehearsal, and these have to be sorted out and dealt with by an already harassed 'wardrobe' (a collective noun used to denote any member of the wardrobe's staff). All the usual things from a split seat in a pair of trousers to a complete separation of a skirt from its bodice, do in fact happen, and very often at the time are not considered amusing by a fraught dancer who is concerned enough as it is with the technical demands of a role without being further encumbered by a flapping or disintegrating costume.

Eventually most things seem to get sorted out. The frayed tempers and prophecies of doom are forgotten as the tension and excitement, always simmering near to boiling before the first night, rises to a peak of nervous anticipation, which releases itself on stage in a burst of energy and enthusiasm in the hope and belief that the audience and the press will, after all, like it.

This year I spent back with the Resident section was also the tricentenary celebration of Shakespeare's birth, in honour of which Sir Fredrick Ashton choreographed the *Midsummer Night's Dream* to the score by Mendelssohn. I was cast as one of the fairies and, although it was not considered to be a totally happy realisation from the *corps de ballet* point of view, personally I rather enjoyed it. At that time anyway, I grasped thankfully at every opportunity to perform.

*La Bayadère* was also new to the Company. It was taught to us

and produced by Rudolph Nureyev, proving him to be as remarkable a teacher as he is a dancer. He revealed an unexpected
degree of patience and although a hard task-master, would always
explain very precisely exactly what he wanted. There was the
additional advantage, of course, of his being able to demonstrate
most beautifully the quality and style he was trying to extract
from us.

*Ondine*, another revival by Sir Fred, once again required a large
cast. It had, many years previously, opened my ears to the
fascinating contemporary score of Heinz Henze. I loved the
choreography for the Ondines (water-sprites) which wove
imaginatively and lyrically into the music, but had never thought
I would actually get the chance to perform it. So my enforced
stay in London had unexpectedly satisfied another long held
desire.

During this year an American film company was compiling
a programme of Royal Ballet 'highlights' which were to be
filmed from the Opera House. Part of the programme included
Act III *Sleeping Beauty* and almost everyone in the Company,
not actually dancing in the variations, formed part of the Court
contingent. I then discovered that the agonies of filming were
even worse than those for television!

Filming started at eight o'clock on Sunday morning, and
continued throughout the day until eight-thirty at night, with
only half-an-hour lunch break. We ended up more exhausted
from standing up all day in heavy court costumes, than if we had
danced every variation.

Somehow I felt the amount of preparation needed, in order to
get anything 'in the can', defeated the so called 'instant' techno-
logical marvel of cinema itself. The whole process is like a
perfectionist's dream, for everything has to be so incredibly
finely balanced and attuned in order to get the right effect that
no one detail can be out of place at any time. This careful attention
to detail, which requires constant repetition of the same two or
three steps, almost extinguishes any spontaneity and life from the
subject.

Maybe this is why ballet nearly always looks so flat and dull on film? The element of chance is missing, which must necessarily bring that extra sense of excitement to a live performance. Instead, one sits back knowing there are going to be no mistakes, or impromptu moments to help establish that very special relationship between the performers, and make the audience aware, and alive to every moment.

But this is a very personal opinion, which many people may not share, and it must be admitted that these films do give everyone the chance of seeing some of the world's most beautiful dancers and exciting choreography.

While I was with the Resident section, I also had the chance at last to enjoy living in London. Alternating performances at the Royal Opera House with the Opera Company did give us the opportunity of free evenings when we could visit other theatres and see visiting companies from abroad. I was also able to meet and make friends with people outside as well as in the Company.

Fortunately these friends' varied lives and interests were a refreshing stimulant, and helped me to keep in touch with the realities of the world outside, instead of remaining depressed by my apparently static position in the Company. Their appreciation of my sort of life also made me very aware of how lucky I was, just to be with the Royal Ballet anyway. A satisfactorily sobering thought, when one tends to get caught up in the driving ambitions of this rather self-centred profession sometimes.

By the end of the year all the necessary arrangements had been made for my transfer back to the Touring section, and I must admit it was with a sense of relief that I packed up at the end of the Season and went on holiday. After a separation of five years I was going to stay with my sister, who was now working very successfully as a dancer, as well as acting as Assistant Choreographer to Michael Kidd.

Everyone thought I was mad to go to New York in the middle of summer, but I loved it. I spent hours wandering around on my own exploring while Susan, my sister, was working. I was also able to sit in on rehearsals sometimes and I found it extremely interesting to watch the very different style and approach of the people involved in commercial work. The atmosphere is much more relaxed and obviously not so purist as ballet. There is not the overpowering sense of dedication, which can be so stifling with ballet, and in fact it made dancing seem much more like fun and less like hard work again!

Commercial dance always sounds horribly derogatory but really it involves just as hard and demanding work as ballet. This is shown nowhere better than in the American musicals. The necessity to continue with regular classes in both classical and modern is something many dancers over here need to understand in order to help raise the standard of work in English musicals.

There is still something of a subconscious stigma attached to commercial work in England. Many dancers still feel they have failed if they do not make the grade in the classic tradition and therefore never put quite the same effort into trying to make a success of modern dance. Whereas in America, where modern dance was really founded at the beginning of the century, there is a far greater sense of tradition, and consequently more respect for this work.

Certainly my respect for it went up in leaps and bounds while I was there. I realised what a lot classical companies can learn from the advances made by modern dance choreographers. It is worth remembering, if for various reasons you cannot become a classical dancer, that modern dance, both through the 'Graham' technique and the commercial theatre's use of modern jazz is an adventurous and contemporary off-shoot of ballet.

Just as Fokine broke with the tradition of the formal Petipa Imperial Ballet style so, in a more radical way possibly, the early American choreographers like Doris Humphery and Martha Graham sought to create a dance style more representative of present-day trends. This was not just happening in America alone of course. A similar reappraisal was taking place in Europe under the direction of Rudolph Laban, Kurt Jooss and Mary Wigman; but the movement really took root and grew in America.

Martha Graham has become perhaps the best-known and accepted modern dance creator, in that her technique has become
a recognised institution in the dance world. It is now almost as
purist in style as ballet, with equally precise and confined limitations. Modern dance, as used in the commercial world, is still a
much more zany experimental affair with only a few well
founded basic techniques of any validity. As a result though it can
lead to some very interesting and original ideas.

New York really brought home to me the fact that dancers
cannot afford to dismiss another faction of their own artistic
medium, for each has something of value to offer the other. To
stay completely bound by any one style is sure to lead to an
explosive situation eventually, for dance, as the art of movement,
needs to use every possible means of bodily expression to fulfil
this purpose.

# 7

## ON THE MOVE AGAIN

### *Soloist and Principal Work*

MY FIRST WEEK back at the beginning of the next season was like a breath of fresh air after the past year. Erling Sunde was teaching with the Company and I found his style and approach to class perfect as far as I was concerned. None of the exercises were rushed. They gave full value and extension to the use of every muscle, a theory of techniques to which I owe a great deal since starting to teach a few years ago.

I also had the added incentive to work with renewed enthusiasm, by being given small solos to understudy, apart from being fully engaged in all the *corps de ballet* work. Once we were out on tour, the opportunity to perform some of these solos came earlier than I had imagined. Many people were plagued by minor injuries, or bouts of 'flu, (which ironically followed hard on the heels of our mass inoculation held in the Royal Retiring Room at the Opera House!) Influenza swept through the Company rapidly laying low the five casts which preceded me for the Garden Fairy in the *Sleeping Beauty* Prologue.

Before I knew what had happened, I found myself written in on the performance schedule one week—and as it happened for the four performances each week for every succeeding week of the remainder of the tour. Sorry as I was for the poor state of health of my friends, I was also ecstatic with delight. I also realised how lucky I was to have such a consistent run of performances, for I really had a chance to become familiar with this short but tricky solo.

It was commonly known as the 'Dick Barton' fairy! Partly
due to the accompanying piece of 'detective-chase' music, and
partly because of the gusto, and attack required to accomplish it,
with any degree of success. At the same time I had the opportunity
to become accustomed to working with a number of different
partners, as my Cavalier changed according to the rest of the
casting for each performance.

Another piece of good news was being cast for one of the two
Leading Wilis in *Giselle*. I had only ever done one performance of
*Giselle* with the Resident Company, and even then my knowledge
of the sequence of steps was a little hazy. I had one call (rehearsal) before I went on as Leading Wili, and have distinct
memories of the first performance. During certain parts of the
ensemble work, where the long arabesque line requires the head
to be level with the arm, I hastily took the opportunity of glancing
upstage underneath my elbow to check I was still going in the
same direction as the rest of the Wilis I was supposedly leading.

The solo itself was easily learned, and I loved the steely coldness
of character which it demanded. I found the force of character
required, made me forget about any technical difficulties, and I so
enjoyed presenting the personality of the role that I was able to
dance with more authority than I felt in some of the similar,
classical, yet less individual roles.

This element of acting was very important to me in my dancing, and became increasingly so as I approached the more principal
roles later on. It also made me very aware how even the smallest
part you play on stage, must be firmly established in your own
mind, with some positive identity. Not only does it make each
ballet more interesting, both for yourself and the audience, but
it is also a very good preventive to weakening nerves.

It was with my initiation into Leading Wilis, that I first started
to dance as a 'pair' with Patricia Ruanne. Nearly all the classical
ballets have a pair of semi-soloists or *coryphées* in one scene or
another. I imagined it was, and still is a way of seeing what
potential a *coryphée* has for solo work, before deciding whether
she can be elevated to the actual rank of soloist.

Working with another person is not quite such an ordeal as doing a completely solo part. Her presence gives a degree of moral support, and there are usually one or two solo spots for each member of the pair. Other examples of the 'pairs' are the 'Miseries' in *Les Sylphides* and the two Big Swans in *Swan Lake* Acts II and IV.

In addition to these pairs there are the many occasions when the 'friends' of the ballerina, usually six or eight girls, often work in pairs. One of these groups of friends attend Princess Aurora in Act I of the *Sleeping Beauty*. But there was a penalty attached to being one of these friends in the production currently in use when I was in the Company: the roses, which four of us had to wear tucked down and concealed within the bodice of our tutus.

It was always a worry having to carry extras of this sort with you while you danced. Forming a vital part of the production, you were always afraid they would pop out at the wrong moment and ruin everything. They did of course on occasion and provided some hilarious moments, so long as you were not the unfortunate victim of circumstance. They admittedly helped to enliven the proceedings when you were performing a ballet time and time again.

Events followed thick and fast throughout the first two tours of that year. Pat (Ruanne) and I did the two Red Girls in *Les Patineurs* adding to our list of 'pairs'. We began to build up a certain rapport with each other so that we could sense each other's balance and timing even with our backs to one another. This rapport is very necessary if you are to acquire a co-ordination and symmetry of line, and as a rule we preferred not to be cast with the other half of another 'pair'.

Somehow one develops the same sense of rhythm, so that even if the conductor suddenly changes the tempo drastically, it is possible still to remain together. We took great pride in this for obviously such close co-operation adds considerably to the whole performance, apart from teaching the value of selflessness when working on stage with someone else whose performance is as important as your own.

We did in fact start *Les Patineurs* with different partners, for it requires a great deal of stamina, and rarely are two new Red Girls put on together for the first time. Our opposite numbers, who had done it many times before, were able to help us fight our way through the first few performances mainly by just showing that they were alive at the end of it!

Later performances brought a greater degree of resilience as we learned where to relax and breathe through it. This is another vital part of learning how to last through and still present a part without exhausting yourself unnecessarily. It is at times like these that an older Company member's advice and experience can be so helpful to someone who is still comparatively new and struggling.

I also began to realise how small a wardrobe one needs to carry on tour. The majority of your time is spent in practice clothes, and the only time you wear anything else is when you are travelling either between the digs and the theatre, or from that week's theatre to the next. This discovery not only brought the relief of carrying round a much lighter and smaller suitcase, but also the simplicity of deciding what to put on in the morning.

We invariably came to London in May for a London Season at the Opera House while the Resident Company toured in America. That year we had a particularly successful Season, and so ended a year, the pattern of which was happily to repeat itself, with variations, for the next two years. Gradually I worked my way through the ranks of *coryphée* to soloist, eventually doing principal roles I would never have dreamed possible.

The opportunity to perform these principal roles also meant I was able to work with some of the most marvellous people I have known. I say people specifically as opposed to dancers, for they were not only exceptional dancers, but the warmest and most sincere individuals whose friendship I value immensely. There is no room for petty jealousies and back-biting in dancing at any level, and particularly in solo roles. Besides, too much of your performance depends on the support and help of others to allow clashes of personality to interfere.

It is a very strange feeling when first you see your name written down on a cast sheet beside a principal role. After the initial shock, more often than not the only thing I could see was the catastrophe the whole performance could become. My imagination ran riot, and without fail my knees turned to water as I vainly tried to imagine myself actually performing in front of an audience. Once the shock has worn off though, the practicalities of learning a part have to be resolved.

It is not always easy to learn a major solo or principal part, for the first thing one has to recognise is that there is more than just the aesthetic and technical demands of the role to be overcome. Tact, surprisingly enough, plays an important part if there is to be any trust and understanding between the teacher and the taught. It is very easy for a dancer's confidence to be shaken, however prestigious his or her position may seem, and Principals therefore are occasionally cautious about personally teaching the parts they are already performing, or are about to perform.

This is natural enough really, when you consider that every promising new-comer constitutes a threat to the always slender hold a Principal has on such a coveted position. It is not that they are unaware of the necessity of being sufficiently well covered by understudies, or even resent the opportunities for younger Company members. In fact it is a positive relief to know that you do not have to struggle nobly on when badly injured or ill.

Much as one would like to feel one is irreplaceable in a certain role, history has proved there will always be a successful substitute ready and waiting to take your place. At the same time there is always the secret fear at the back of your mind that ultimately you could well remain ousted from your position altogether.

The fear is very easy to understand and, even with the excitement of starting to learn principal roles, there is an equal awareness of the inevitability of being placed in the same situation yourself one day. You therefore respect the experience and seniority of those already ahead of you, and do not assume an attitude of important assertiveness which can so easily develop from tactlessness or insensitive actions.

It is impossible to harbour any resentment, or withhold information when you know and can sympathise with the problems facing someone else. I was always grateful to the people who taught and helped me. They pointed out the physical and emotional problems all the time, and later, when I handed on roles to younger dancers I realised that one almost had a duty to one's profession to do this. If you cannot hand on the experience you have gained, both for yourself and from other people, it does become a very selfish way of life.

Ballet would also lose a lot of its tradition, for dancers have always inherited and handed on the knowledge gained by previous generations. It would be impossible for ballet or dance to have made the progress it has without this close relationship between dancers, who never withhold any of the secrets gained through either hard work or heritage.

Another aspect of withholding, on a much more emotional level, is that you cannot easily conceal any part of your personality when you are on stage, for it will always be reflected in the performances you produce. Absolute honesty, both with yourself and the audience, is very necessary if you are to present a fully rounded performance of depth and sincerity. The very nature of dance is to communicate in a visual sense, and one's every gesture and expression must be clearly recognised and understood within oneself before the audience can be asked to believe in it. Although this may seem far removed from the actual learning of principal roles, it is in fact a point which has to be recognised early on if you are to make a success of being a Principal dancer.

A great deal can be learned initially, by watching the various interpretations of a role. Usually there is more than one person performing it regularly, which gives you the opportunity to compare, and draw your own conclusions as to how you feel about already established interpretations. These give you something on which to base your own style, and interpretation, which should be both complementary to yourself and the nature of the role itself.

Even though a role may be a straightforward classical variation there are still certain accents and nuances which make a difference to the quality and general impression of the piece. It is essential to discover where the light and shade lies in a variation, in order to give it depth and content. Ultimately, the ideal is to develop an interpretation which becomes something quite unique to you yourself, but still within the context of the ballet as a whole.

There are also the very practical, as well as the more aesthetic considerations of working on a role. A tremendous degree of self-discipline is required in order to control the effect of the unavoidable nerves when you first perform. Controlling your nerves is really a question of will-power. It needs a careful, analysed approach to each section of the part, whereby you break it down into phrases as you would with a piece of music. It will fall into a series of natural breaks once you really study the steps, and most important of all is the resulting knowledge you acquire of where and how to breathe.

This can be worked out in relation to where you can afford to relax or rest before a particularly demanding section which requires all your concentration. You learn to think ahead by doing this so that you are never taken unawares by something either fast moving and tricky, or slow and controlled. It is at moments like these that complete calm is essential or panic steps in, and you start fighting a losing battle to regain control.

The other vital factor in combating nerves, is stamina. Nervous tension saps a good deal of your energy, so it is necessary to build up extra reserves. You then have something to boost what would normally be sufficient. The only way to build up these reserves, is by doggedly pushing yourself to the extremes in rehearsals. By going on and on mastering the technical aspects until you are so exhausted you feel you will burst. Then the disciplined technique becomes so firmly implanted in your normal reactions, that your body produces it spontaneously when your mind is too numb to think clearly.

This not only builds up the stamina to a degree whereby you find you can run through the whole piece two or three times consecutively—which is often the case at dress-rehearsals—but also leaves you with the freedom and confidence you require to concentrate almost entirely on the interpretation you wish to give during the performance. Apart from this though you find that you need every ounce of this increased stamina when the time comes for the performance on stage, for through sheer nervous tension alone, you are as exhausted at the end of it as if you had done it six times over!

One of the first principal roles I performed was Queen of the Wilis in Act II *Giselle*. It is a role which requires a steely coldness and control at the beginning, and a good degree of elevation later on when you never seem to stop jumping. Worst of all though, there is no point at which you can collapse into the wings to puff and pant for air following all this exertion. Instead you have to retain all the dignity, authority and self-control befitting the character, and remain standing regally at the side of the stage for all the mime sections until the end of the Act.

This particular role was fraught with other hazards in addition to all the purely aesthetic and technical requirements. First, there was the problem of my own veil. I entered *bourré-ing* diagonally across the stage covered in a long veil similar to an ordinary bridal veil—indicating that Wilis are young girls who died tragically on the eve of their wedding nights. A glaring spotlight seemingly directed straight at my eyes prevented me from seeing anything too clearly, let alone the other side of the stage, while the gauzy net of the veil additionally hampered my vision.

Having successfully reached the opposite wing the veil had to be quickly removed so that I could immediately return on the next phrase of music. The second exit was also followed by my immediate return, armed this time with a pair of silver birch twigs in either hand. They were representative of a divine and mystical power, which cast a spell on the place where the Wilis were to dance at night.

These had to be adroitly thrown with a flick of the wrist into the wings—one either side of the stage. They very often missed fire altogether and would un-magically hit the wing with a resounding thud, or more embarrassingly still, catch in the net of the dress, consequently falling limply to the ground a matter of inches away. They then had to be unconcernedly, but strategically kicked towards the wing at some point!

There was also a particularly harrowing moment shortly after all the exertions later on, when Giselle makes her first appearance as a Wili. She also is veiled as she rises from the tomb and must appear before the Queen to be unveiled. Apart from the problem of trying to recover my breath, I also had to start listening intently to the music between my finishing and Giselle's appearance. At a very specific point in the music, we would approach one another, and it was up to me to whisk the veil off in one movement.

This is no easy feat when you consider the fine mesh of the net resting on the forest of hair-pins and small floral head-dress on Giselle's head. I was almost more nervous for this part than for any of the dancing I had previously performed. One false move and the whole veil could become entangled on her head and prove absolutely inextricable. Invariably we would have a trial run before the curtain went up on the Act, and whoever was dancing Giselle would try to adjust the veil to exactly the right angle.

Whenever possible the casting was arranged so that we were of comparable heights—the Queen preferably being a little taller than Giselle. This was not just for the sole reason of the veil removal, although it helped considerably, but because the extra height lent an air of authority and command to the role of the Queen, and by contrast, places Giselle in an even more ethereal and fragile light.

One was able to build up a certain rapport over a period of time. Because of the limited casting system and because each Giselle only worked with one or two Albrechts, the resulting trio of Principals were able to solidify and establish their relationships both in context with the ballet and with the individual characters.

It was very interesting to note the different emotions the various Giselles evoked during all the mime sections between herself and the Queen. It was really very indicative of the sort of empathy

felt between two people on stage, with regard to their understanding and interpretation of the role. It was something one
could feel not just in connection with oneself, but also sense very
strongly between other casts in both roles.

It reaches the point, where one is reluctant to have to change
from a successful combination, and it always made me extra
nervous having to perform with someone with whom I could not
feel this magical rapport. It also made the performance much harder
work than usual, as it required extra concentration and effort to
project the drama of the story.

It is amazing the difference this relationship can create, and how
much their interdependence can strengthen the performance
as a whole. As a Principal one realises the responsibilities one has
to the rest of the cast, for they react to your strengths and weak-
nesses. The Principals very often act as a barometer to the success
or failure of a ballet. The degree of their involvement with one
another as the characters they are portraying is sensed and re-
sponded to by the rest of the dancers. I always feel that I was
extremely fortunate in having in my view, some of the finest
partners, both technically and dramatically.

When I first played the Wife in *The Invitation* by Kenneth
Macmillan, I had to work with two partners, the Husband,
Adrian Grater, and the Boy, David Wall. They helped me immensely, not just through their partnering, but their acting as
well. They gave performances from which one always had something substantial to play off, and so a chain reaction was set up.

In this particular ballet one had to establish several different
relationships very clearly for there are four Principal characters,
the Young Girl being the fourth in the quartet. Each character
has a very definite and strong reaction to each of the other three.
A sensitivity towards the individual interpretations is essential for
the emotional conflicts to become apparent to an audience.

I was very fortunate in that Pat Ruanne played the Girl and
what we were able to develop in the conflict of the two characters
was really an extension of our having worked already very closely
together as a 'pair'. In later performances I also worked with

Doreen Wells as the Girl and Hendrik Davel as the Boy. Although both equally compelling in performance, they required a subtly different attitude on my behalf to make our interpretations correspond each with the other's. They too had to adjust to me as a character, but these small differences really only go towards making each performance as fresh and alive as possible, and in no way detract from the total.

# 8

## COSTUME, MAKE-UP AND OTHER PRACTICAL DETAILS

TWO OTHER POINTS which Principals have to be particularly conscious of, although it applies of course to all members of a Company, are their costumes and make-up. Make-up is something you learn to use immediately you enter a Company, slowly improving the overall effect as the weeks pass by. Once again older Company members are extremely helpful in assisting very green juniors, showing them how best to present themselves to make the most of their individual characteristics.

There are several basic rules regarding a straightforward stage make-up, but in the end a lot depends on your physical features as to how and where the make-up is actually applied. The lighting for ballets makes a tremendous difference regarding the colour of 'base'—literally basic foundation—which you use. A blue light, as used in white ballets, like *Les Sylphides* or act II *Giselle*, needs an almost yellow/green tinge in the make-up, as opposed to the normal pink/brown, in order to combat the otherwise purplish hues induced by blue on pink.

Character make-up is yet another extension which requires tremendous care and understanding of the effects created by colours, shading and lines. The major mistake made by most newcomers is an over-enthusiastic approach to the whole problem, which results in heavy applications of multi-coloured grease sticks, especially around the eyes. Unfortunately the result of this approach, is a positively mask-like appearance on stage, which effectively blocks out any facial communication with the audience. The exact reverse of what was originally intended.

Make-up really is an art, and after you have spent some hours studying your own face in the mirror week after week, you will begin to understand just how much artistic skill it takes to transform your amazingly lop-sided and extraordinary features into a presentable appearance! Nobody who has spent so many hours surveying their own physiognomy is ever likely to fall prone to vanity. There is always a flaw to be found somewhere, which becomes a constant bone of contention with its owner when making-up.

As a student you may receive a certain amount of instruction regarding both hair and make-up. Invariably though, you learn the finer points of both these arts once you are in a company. The shape of the hair is often as important as the colour and shading of make-up for suggesting character.

First of all one has to achieve a flattering shape in 'classical' (the traditional style of centre parting with the hair swathed over both ears into a bun at the back), or straightforward hair styles, before attempting more involved or elaborate arrangements. It is also necessary to understand why some of the underpinning and structure work of these hair styles is done. Unless you know how to fix your hair really securely for the more basic styles, it is not nearly so easy to anchor your own or false hair when creating a less sculptured form.

A 'classical' can form the basic shape for a hair style in some ballets onto which various pieces of additional hair are attached for the purposes of changing character. In some of the bigger ballet companies here, and nearly all those on the Continent, you receive, on joining, a set of standard pieces of extra hair which are specially matched to your own hair colour.

These usually consist of bunches of ringlets, and a bird's-nest —this is the now familiar cluster of rolled curls worn on the crown of the head. Sometimes a long switch is also included, and a half-head—a length of hair woven to a base which is placed half-way back on the head—for those whose own hair is too short to make into a 'classical'.

The bird's-nest is usually worn on the top, towards the back of the head to add height and elegance to a head-dress, or to provide an illusion of greater fullness to the actual hairdressing.

It can also be worn on the side of the head over a classical to appear beneath a period hat in a thick bunch of curls, resembling a courtesan's dressed wig. The bird's-nest needs careful pulling into shape at the side, so that it does not look as though it has been slapped on like a pancake. In fact this applies every time extra pieces of hair are worn.

Dame Ninette once summed it up beautifully by stating that we had 'no sense of period'. She was undoubtedly right, for I later saw exactly what she meant when young inexperienced dancers would appear with mere apologies for a period hairstyle, looking as though they had been to an old-fashioned crimping parlour, rather than creating a coiffure befitting a courtier.

The necessity to become a competent and creative hairdresser is obvious! Having accomplished these relatively few straight-forward hairdressings, you can then form a structurally firm foundation for more stylised arrangements. This basic knowledge also ensures that any style you may create will be both flattering and secure.

Wigs are in many ways much simpler to deal with, although the glue required for sticking the gauze foundation on the fore-head can be quite painful. Spirit gum is the usual solution used, as it can be easily removed with surgical spirit, though continual use tends to make you feel as though you have been scalped. Boys probably have more wigs to wear than girls, as well as occasional moustaches and side-burns, and I never cease to be amazed at the difference these additions make to a person. It is quite intriguing to see how personalities change and acquire mannerisms of the character they are portraying, when wigged and be-whisk-ered.

Tights, ribbons, and shoes, are generally the three items of your costume for which you are personally responsible. Their condi-tion and appearance are very important, being subject to close scrutiny from the audience, who will be particularly watching feet and legs for the majority of the performance.

The lighting conditions I mentioned earlier also completely alter the colour of tights. Your own stock of tights therefore has to be planned and maintained in order that you always have the right tights for the right occasion. To achieve this it is often necessary to supplement the colours made available by manufacturers with your own combinations of dye colouring—cold tea being a well tried life restorer for old tights.

The blue light makes a pair of already deep pink tights absolutely puce in colour, and these appearing from beneath a white dress tend to give you a comic resemblance to a mincing pink flamingo. A brilliant white light however completely absorbs the strength of any colour and can reduce a naturally pale pair of tights to near whiteness. This conversely makes your legs look rather like a pair of shapeless bolsters.

Deciding on the colour of tights to be worn for a performance is really a question of sensible deduction. It is also an integral part of your involvement with the role you are performing.

Generally, the more unethereal or un-romantic a part you play, the deeper and more natural becomes the shade of your skin, and therefore your tights. This applies to all exposed areas that are supposed to be flesh coloured, so in order to achieve a total image it is important to relate the rest of your make-up to the colour you have chosen for your legs.

Taking care to think along these lines also helps you in your conception of the character, and gradually it assumes an identity, rather than remaining a stiff cardboard cut-out. Your enthusiasm for making even the most mundane 'villager' come alive is pleasurably increased when you realise that you are, after all, projecting an extension of yourself into an imaginary field.

The total image also extends to your feet, which should blend in colour with your legs as naturally as they do when bare. The most obvious visual break usually occurs round the ankles, where the ribbons cross and tie. One way to overcome this is by dyeing batches of ribbon at the same time as the tights. This can result in complications later though, unless you are brilliantly organised, and always sure of having *pointe* shoes in the right condition and degree of softness, or hardness, required by the ballet, together with the appropriate ribbons sewn on.

Another relatively simple method of solving the problem is to rub pancake, or cheap compressed powder, onto the ribbons as required. Both preparations wash out very easily and do not permanently affect the ribbons with the colour used. Darker shades are most easily applied in this way. Toning down the colour is more simply achieved by patting talcum powder or loose face powder over the ribbons. This also reduces any risk of shininess. Even powdered resin can be used as a last resort, should you arrive in the wings and find that the light affects either tights or ribbons, so creating opposing shades.

The actual shoes can also be treated with shaded powders, in the same way as the ribbons. In fact for any white ballet the shoes are always dusted over with white powder, to take away the pink shiny glow of the satin. It is better not to use pancake on shoes as the application with a wet sponge tends to shrink them—an uncomfortable and sometimes disastrous discovery to make when they have dried, and you are about to put them on for a performance. Alternatively, it can provide just the right degree of effective treatment for older slightly baggy shoes that have achieved a state of comfort you are loath to sacrifice.

There is nothing worse than the sound of clip-clopping *pointe* shoes thundering across the stage during a performance, and it is always a problem to know how best to deaden the sound without losing the strength of the blocking. One rather drastic method is banging the bottom of the shoe's toes on a hard surface, such as concrete. But this does tend to split or crack the blocking of the *pointe* in the most vital area, especially when they are fresh from the factory, and the glue is still very brittle, if it has not had time to mature and strengthen sufficiently. A more effective means is to dampen lightly the underside of the blocking next to the sole, which muffles the sound without ruining the *pointe*.

On the other hand, restoring life to old shoes is equally important. I always found it well worth the short amount of time required—if only to save the state of my feet. There is generally constant chafing when breaking in new shoes which have not yet accustomed their shape to the various and unique bumps on your feet. This can be helped by breaking down very gently the stiffness in the blocking on the top and to the side of the shoes with your hands.

Shoes that can no longer be cleaned into a presentable condition, are well used during rehearsals with the aid of shellac—a hardening agent which dries overnight when poured into the toe of the shoe.

Most of these problems apply to girls obviously, as the boys have very little to worry about concerning the care of shoes and tights for performance. Tights are usually supplied by the Wardrobe, and the only thing left to do, is to sew elastic onto shoes. Bostick is widely used for glueing on the heels when elastic is impractical, and it is really almost safer than elastic, as the foot cannot then walk out of the shoe—an agonising event which can ruin a performance for both audience and artist alike. It is, after all, rather unmagical to see a large, shapeless size 9 left abandoned centre stage!

As far as the rest of your costume is concerned, unless it is a completely new production, you wear your predecessor's costume with alterations where necessary. Even Principals, particularly young Principals, rarely have a costume especially made for them when they go into a new role. You can well find yourself wearing a costume that once belonged to somebody who left the Company many years previously, and in fact there is almost a degree of superstitious good luck attached to the costume you take over, depending on who last wore it.

It is certainly not a question of being fobbed off with second-hand goods, for one feels that some of the magic created by the person who was in that costume, might rub off on you in performance. A great deal of care is taken over costume alterations for Principals, to ensure that they fit, are comfortabe to work in, and flattering to the wearer. I don't think that I ever had a Principal costume made especially for me, but on the contrary, I felt very proud to inherit some of the costumes and wigs I wore.

But it is marvellous when a new costume is made for you for a new production, and you feel particularly good on the first night, knowing that you do not have to worry about any possibility of gaping fastenings or drooping hem-lines. It is also rather nice to know that the cardboard box containing wigs or head-dresses and the label on the inside of the costume, will go into posterity bearing your name as the original wearer.

Costumes are kept in store for years if there is any possibility of the ballet being revived at a later date, and I remember when we revived *Mamselle Angot* a ballet by Leonard Massine, the original costumes were brought out of storage from some fifteen to twenty years back!

The worst thing is sharing a costume, although this has to happen a great deal because of the immense cost of making some of the costumes. However, it can be very unpleasant to receive a costume worn at the previous matinee, still soaking wet, for the evening performance. It is not quite so bad having to clamber into your own sweaty costume, but someone else's always seems far worse.

All these considerations contribute towards the ever-present fear and excitement as each new role is approached, rehearsed and finally performed, and is something that you never forget. The excitement especially makes all the other hardships worthwhile, for like any other physical pain, once it is past it is soon forgotten. Eventually, when I could no longer continue dancing, at least I had the memories and consoling knowledge of having achieved ambitions and dreams beyond my wildest thoughts.

The memory of one role in particular—the Wife in Macmillan's *The Invitation* was to remain especially dear to me. It provided the opportunity of confirming my belief that the combination of a strong acting element with dance, achieves the most satisfactory extension of ballet today. If I had not had the chance to perform just one comparatively contemporary role as satisfying as this, I should always have felt I had missed experiencing the sense of fulfilment which every dancer needs to know.

Without wishing to sound sentimental, it also taught me the

increasing sense of humility one feels at the recognition so warmly shown and given by the public. They are so willing for you to succeed simply by pleasing them that, as time passes, one becomes more than ever aware of the responsibility one has towards them. Their appreciation shown in both applause and bouquets is warmly received and gratefully aknowledged.

Once again the hard work and daily grind is forgotten as the applause begins, and even the youngest member of the *corps* is made abundantly conscious of the acknowledgement of their contribution to the performance as a whole. The shared elation at the end of a perfect performance is indescribable, and is the nearest thing I know to a pure and uncomplicated union of spirits.

# 9

## TIME OUT FROM THE THEATRE

### *Adjusting to a Change of Career*

THE END OF MY THIRD YEAR with the Touring Company was also to bring the end of my career as a dancer. It had been a marvellous year with a Continental tour to Finland, Scandinavia, Brussels and Germany, followed by a very successful London Season. I had been increasingly worried though by an old back injury which, despite treatment and rest, would not seem to improve.

Admittedly treatment had only been spasmodic because of my continual touring and the knowledge that to be off for any length of time at this point in my career could jeopardise the good rate of progress I had been making so far.

The condition became worse and worse though, and nothing seemed to do the trick. Eventually my right leg became quite numb, and X-rays revealed that the spinal column had partially collapsed at the base causing two vertabrae to fall lopsidedly onto one another. They had gradually worked together until finally a shallow groove had been worn on the underneath one. The ever decreasing disc in between left no room for the central nervous system to pass through, and it could not escape pressure from above.

This is what caused the painful numbing effect. The fact that my right leg was a good three quarters of an inch longer than the left was another contributory factor to the whole problem. It seemed amazing that such a chronic condition had all been sparked off from a simple fall some three or four years earlier when I had landed on the base of my spine.

X-rays then had revealed no physical defect, but over the years the increasing degree of concentrated work, particularly in roles of elevation, had aggravated the already weakened structure of discs and vertabrae. I should not, perhaps, have been so afraid of losing further promotion and work when I first became aware that my back was injured, for ultimately every dancer is responsible for controlling the amount of work he or she does.

Unfortunately though, whichever way you look at it a dancer is always an expendable item within a Company, and whatever course of action you take, it remains a gamble whether you will gain or lose in the end as a dancer.

Perhaps it is worth considering here, the point that there are always two sides to an argument concerning loss or gain. Eventually, I was left with the choice of carrying on dancing with the help of massage, heat-treatment and osteopathy, for maybe another year or two, at a decreased level of work, and probably worsening the condition until I was semi-crippled. Or I could stop working immediately and know I would be able to continue living a reasonably normal physical life.

It seemed to me that to forsake everything for the pleasure, or pain of two more years dancing was a very high price to pay for an acknowledgedly transitory phase of life. I was still young and had the rest of my life ahead of me. It seemed morally wrong somehow to sacrifice that life, for what amounted to sheer self-indulgence and egotism. Apart from this, although like most dancers my level of pain was of a much higher toleration than that of the average person, I had really reached my limit now.

This higher level of pain was due to the fact that the whole process of becoming a dancer is a very physical and painful procedure. Ballet, or indeed any form of modern dance training is really a masochistic form of torture. There is the unnatual struggle to turn the legs out from the hips (particularly hard for boys); the stretching and flexing of unwilling joints and muscles, and finally, for girls the continual pain of having to stagger around on the *pointes* of your feet, as though you were born to perform such eccentricities!

I could not imagine what it would be like any more to continue this daily battle with my body, which had now rebelled in every way it knew how. So the decision was made in favour of a longer life and a shorter career. There seemed to be a lot of advantages in a longer life with the chance to explore other interests and ambitions despite my sorrow at leaving ballet. But I had no idea what I was going to do next!

Since everything in the way of work with the Company had pointed towards a continuing success for at least a few more years, I had not really considered anything else. I had thought of various ideas in a vague sort of way, bearing in mind myself the remarks I made earlier about the brevity and frailty of a dancer's life. So at least I had some idea of what I did and did not want to do.

I was offered the possibility of teaching, or acting as repetiteur with the Company, but at that moment I could not honestly face the prospect of standing aside and watching other people dance in the ballets I still longed to do. I was afraid that if I did accept the position I might become very bitter about my circumstances, and spoil what had been a memorable and enjoyable part of my life. At the same time I had to admit that I was loth to leave entirely, the environment of the theatre.

I began to think back to the training I had received in acting at Elmhurst, and that maybe now I could put other facets of it to use. I had gained so much general knowledge of the theatre now, through touring, that the transition seemed a fairly natural one. Obviously I would need to renew voice production lessons after such a gap, but otherwise everything seemed to be in favour of this extension. Another possibility to be considered was training for producing or directing within the theatre, or television.

Gradually though, I was to learn that unfortunately the Arts are not as closely knit as one would like to think, when it comes to changing jobs. Apparently the experience you gain in one field is of absolutely no value anywhere else. A depressing state of affairs, which I am afraid only accents the single-mindedness of most sections of the performing arts. Hopefully, this will change with time, as the theatre becomes much more of a total experience, incorporating all elements of voice and movement.

Already there is a trend in this direction whereby a multitude of talents are required, rather than just one accomplished technique. Performers are no longer confined to the specific roles of acting, singing, or dancing, but use all three techniques rolled into one to extend their vocabulary both as performers and people.

I am thinking specifically of Peter Brook's International Centre for Theatre Research, which is almost a reversion to the art of the *Commedia Dell' Arte,* or theatre as it was first performed. In a lesser degree though some of these experiments, which Mr. Brook has carried out, have already been incorporated into productions by other producers and choreographers thinking along the same lines.

As you can imagine, the mental adjustment from thinking of ballet as my career, to acting or producing was not as sudden and complete as it sounds. I had never quite abandoned hope of dancing again and secretly I was sure that after a rest all would be well. However having done the 'Grand Tour' of Harley Street, and many other recommended people besides, I finally came to accept that possibly the unvarying opinions of so many doctors could not be wrong.

I made one final effort after six months' rest, to start dancing again, but as soon as the first few careful classes were accomplished I knew instinctively that my back was never going to stand the technical strain and demands of ballet, and sure enough the numbing pains soon returned.

Finally I made a small breakthrough in the acting world. It followed a frustrating and worrying period of being out of work, and consequently out of money, during the six months of physical rest. This sudden employment was to bring home to me very forcibly the perilous state in which a dancer is permanently placed, from the financial point of view.

Until then I had not realised how secure a dancer is within a Company compared with a free-lance or commercial dancer. We had a regular annual contract, with specified rates of salary which were renewed almost unquestioningly, so guaranteeing a set income for the year. Only by a free choice of leaving the Company, or a terminating injury, is this security threatened.

Freelance dancers though are always totally dependent on the work available and their suitability for it, which means there can be long periods out of work. Both lives do provide the chance to save, one in small consistent amounts when on a regular contract, the other on a more sporadic basis as and when the work and money are available. But seldom do either group think of the need for saving while actually in work.

Tax rebates, a welcome bonus when you are out of work, are only acquired through being on the P.A.Y.E. system, which is very rarely used in the theatre. Supplementary allowances through the National Insurance work on the same principle, so all a dancer normally received at this time was the standard rate of sickness benefit or unemployment. The onus lay entirely with the individual for having something extra to fall back on in times of distress.

Private insurance begins to assume an aspect of importance in the light of these facts, even taking into account the present Resettlement Scheme. Any good insurance company will help you sort out the best type of policy for your requirements, and it is really a point worth considering when you embark on such a precarious career.

Equity's insurance can cover you for certain occurrences, but like many 'general' insurances they can slither through your fingers, as strange, obscure clauses of law are wielded to leave you unprotected and consequently penniless. The best thing to do, is to make doubly sure of receiving financial benefit by insuring independently as well—usually at a very moderate fee.

Unfortunately my foray into the acting world was not to last long either. It was a children's travelling theatre company which toured round southern England playing to schools once or twice a day. The salary was a pittance, but at least for the moment I was actually working again.

There were only five of us, and we were responsible for everything. Unloading the van in which we travelled, setting up the scenery and lighting, unpacking costumes, and operating the tape recorder and 'tabs' (curtains) from the wings when not actively engaged in performing on the stage. The whole process then had to be repeated in reverse as we set off for the next school, or village hall.

Obviously humping heavy scenery and hampers of costumes did little to enhance the condition of my back; likewise the continual bumpy travelling in the very old dormobile van. The other three actors apart from the one who drove, were all extremely kind, and insisted I travelled up front instead of being squashed in amongst the scenery at the back—even though it did mean balancing my feet on a biscuit tin.

This was strategically placed to cover the hole in the floor through which a healthy gale used to whistle, together with the odd snow flurry during January. Two or three months of this though completely undid any of the good achieved through my previous rest, and sadly I had to accept that because of my back I was just not capable any more of dealing with these hard conditions.

I made one last effort to stay at least vaguely associated with the performing arts, as I thought, by modelling. I was considered unsuitable for either photographic, or couturier modelling because my ballet training again was regarded as a disadvantage rather than an asset at the time. The phase in fashion then was for a rather gamin type, without much sophistication of movement, and I moved too gracefully or consciously even when I tried not to!

However, when I did actually do a fashion show where they were specifically looking for models who could move and act as well, the boredom was so indescribable that I would never have been happy doing it anyway. And so I decided I was better off searching elsewhere.

Once I had exhausted all attempts to continue working in the theatre, I felt it was imperative to gain some sort of commercial qualification so that at least I was capable of the relatively simple duties of a typist. After a condensed course in touch-typing I started to look around for something which, if I must type, would at least be of an interesting and constructive nature.

The ideal opportunity presented itself almost immediately through the columns of *The Times* 'Women's Appointments', of which I had by now become an avid reader. The job was private secretary to a wine importer, but working from my own home rather than office premises. I have always been very interested in wine, and this seemed a good way of learning more about the subject.

I had a considerable amount of translation to do from French to English and *vice versa*, and on the whole it was a very interesting job. But my employer was a little eccentric, to say the least. As his private secretary, I was responsible for handling his own personal affairs. These were many and varied, but nearly all were extremely complex. Eventually, what had started as a part-time job became a frustrating and time-consuming occupation. And so, a little regretfully, I extricated myself from further involvement.

The situation had had its advantages even so, for the eccentric but engaging character of my employer, and the diversity of his interests, apart from the wine trade, had begun to arouse within me the feeling for another creative element which I had hitherto rather neglected. It occurred to me that such an experience had provided more than ample material for a short story. So I began seriously to consider the possibility of writing.

The more I thought about it the more I realised how writing could constructively release all the thoughts and ideas that had passed through my mind over the last few months. Since being detached from the immediate surroundings of the ballet, I had given a great deal of thought to my profession, and its artistic importance in the world today. Now I felt that perhaps I could continue to share and expand what I had recently discovered.

Together with the hard, practical experience of having been a dancer, I could divert these thoughts into some written form of communication which other dancers could recognise and relate to on both a practical and personal level. I began therefore, not by writing a story about my amusing wine importer—but by organising and consolidating my thoughts and knowledge on the whole background of dance and ballet. I did this in the form of a thesis, through which I explored the original conception and purpose of ballet, and compared it with its present value and state of development.

This was to take me many months of hard, but fascinating research, apart from the effort to find and achieve a consistent style of writing. At the same time I was continuing the struggle with the various official bodies of the Health and Social Securities Services, regarding my National Health Insurance claims for compensation under the rather incongruous heading of Industrial Injuries. As I mentioned before, the normal forms of insurance are very rarely of much use to a dancer.

The only reason I persevered over a period of two years, was because of a determination to break the impasse usually reached between theatricals and the Social Security officials. I felt that if I could create a precedent it would form a basis from which other dancers might be able to act when placed in a similar position.

There was a vast amount of paper-work, interviews and examinations to be endured, but I felt it was worth it. Eventually, having appealed against the initial assessment of my loss of ability to continue working in my profession, which was placed at £12.00 (twelve £s!) for life, I won my case and achieved a more realistic assessment. It may have come two years too late, to help me weather financially the difficult transition period to other work, but at least I had made my point, and hopefully other professionals may also benefit from this effort in the future.

There is now a Dancers' Resettlement Bureau, supported by a fund. This has been set up to assist dancers who are injured or about to retire. Advice about retraining and government grants is available—also, in special cases, financial assistance.*

In the meantime I still had to live, so I cast around yet again to see what other abilities I might extend, and put to good use. The fact that I was interested in wine was no accident, for wine and

* The Dancers' Resettlement Fund, c/o Mrs. Margaret Wilson, The Arts Council, 105 Piccadilly, London SW1.

food go together, and cooking was a very favourite pastime. A friend of mine, who was a Cordon Bleu cook, suggested I should try cooking professionally.

She knew my cooking well from being a regular guest and said she would be perfectly prepared to recommend me to a past employer. He was and still is Editor to a well-known national newspaper, and it was necessary for him and his wife to entertain formally about once or twice a month. This required the constant presence of both host and hostess throughout the evening which meant they really needed the services of an experienced cook.

I would discuss the menu with his wife a few days before the evening and we would agree on what had to be bought. Normally she would have the bulk of the shopping delivered to the house, and I baked the bread and bought fresh cheeses from Soho to take with me on the day. Then it was merely a question of preparing and cooking during the evening while the butler relieved me of the various dishes for each course. The whole venture was really a great success and they were marvellous people to work for. Also I was doing something I really enjoyed, for I find cooking is as much a creative art as any of the more usually accepted subjects.

My purpose in mentioning all this though is really to show how many different ways there are of channelling one's creative instincts, if one source of inspiration is curtailed. Life becomes so much more pleasurable if your interests are not centred on one sole objective, and I have often thought that in fact my injury was a blessing in disguise. It gave me the chance to re-discover all the things that had been pushed to one side in the scramble to reach the top of just one, very precarious ladder.

That is not to say that throughout this time I had forgotten, or dismissed the idea of working in the theatre. I spoke earlier of the love/hate relationship one develops for ballet, and how impossible it is, once trapped, to fully escape its charms. I had to admit to myself that, given the chance, I would go back to the theatre: sometime, somehow, for it had become so very much a part of my life. I felt that somewhere there was still a region within which I could work.

The writing I had been doing was now completed, and by way of introduction to my style and work I took the plunge and started to send it out to various publishers and theatre friends for comments and opinions. I soon discovered that as far as general publishers are concerned, ballet has a very small market, and although I had much helpful and constructive advice, the publishing value of such material was nil. However, I contacted Mary Clarke, Editor of *The Dancing Times* to see whether she had any suggestions concerning the possibility of my working for the magazine.

This contact was in fact to start up a chain reaction which eventually led me back into the theatre, and made all the hard work and worries of the previous two years seem like time well-spent, and experience well-gained.

# 10

## RETURNING WITH A DIFFERENCE:

### *The Coliseum and Contemporary Dance*

DANCERS ON THE WHOLE it seems are not renowned for putting pen to paper. Probably because the time and opportunity are always sadly lacking, unless one makes a really determined effort to make time; and even that is not always possible. It makes me wish, very forcibly sometimes that ballet was not such an all-devouring involvement, for it would be nice to think that future ballet critics and authors could be drawn from the ranks of experienced dancers, whose mastery of the English language is equal to their ballet technique.

I may be biased but I am sure their criticisms would be far more constructive than those we often have at present, and could do much to raise both the morale and even the standards of dancers and choreographers. At the moment, they are so often unfairly condemned by those whose knowledge of the conceptual and technical problems involved in presenting a ballet is rather more limited.

Perhaps my enjoyment in writing for and about dancers will help to encourage others. I hope maybe they too will gain the confidence to develop writing abilities which have previously been suppressed because of lack of time, or stimulation. It would certainly do much to enrich the literary aspect of the ballet world.

I wrote to Mary Clarke, and was amazed to find that she was very encouraging. She was both surprised and pleased to find a dancer as willing to write about her profession as perform in it.

I arranged to meet her shortly afterwards to discuss a series for the magazine. Having decided on a form and shape for the series, I started work on a trial piece to see if it was suitable.

It was, and from that grew a series of fourteen articles called *Things They Forget to Tell You*. This was directed towards students and young professionals just starting to work and live in London, and hoping eventually to graduate into a Company.

The purpose of the series was to point out all the little things which are no longer considered tremendous obstacles or difficulties by anybody who has been in the profession for any length of time, but which I remembered all too well as making life miserable for any newcomer. At the same time I tried to make the whole series fairly light-hearted. It is often a great help to be able to laugh at yourself, and at the dilemmas in which you can find yourself on occasion, rather than let them add to the already melodramatic situations so easily found in a dancer's day-to-day life.

The articles were apparently received quite well, and I certainly enjoyed writing them. With their appearance the tide of events began to turn at last, and I really began to feel I was finding a niche for myself, connected with the work I most enjoyed. Then, almost as an extra bonus, and as a direct result of the articles, I was offered a job actually working within the theatre again.

Pauline Grant had recently taken over the direction of Sadler's Wells Opera Ballet, now based at the Coliseum. In so doing she had entirely changed the approach and character of their style of work. They were to be known in future as the 'Movement Group', and were to play a much more integral role in the Opera Productions. This meant a great deal of reformation both in the structure and personnel of the Group, and for this she needed the help of an assistant.

She had read some of my articles and liked them. By sheer coincidence she had at the same time been in contact with Elmhurst, to see if they could recommend anyone suitable for the job of assistant. They, unknown to me, suggested my name, and that she felt meant that fate had more or less taken a hand in making the decision for her. We met, and after talking for a while found we both seemed to agree on the principles concerning the growth and development of the Movement Group.

I started working on a three-month trial basis, to see whether it was a practical venture. This meant working in conjunction with the choreographers and producers during the full production rehearsals for which the Group was required: as well as rehearsing them myself, independently from the singers, for any particular dance sequences they did in an opera. In addition I was to give classical classes to the Group. There was also the administrative side, which involved helping Pauline to construct the call sheets, and casting details for each production, and type any necessary correspondence from our office.

The most difficult part was taking the classes initially, for many of the newly formed Group had had either a very rudimentary training, or no training at all in dance. They were assessed more on their ability to move and act, rather than as potential dancers. This was obviously a very valid standpoint when you consider that the majority of the work they had to do was in conjunction with operatic productions. But it did cause something of an imbalance in classes.

The girls were nearly all of a fairly reasonable standard, and in fact there was never any shortage of good girl dancers who could also act. The boys presented a bigger problem. Most of them had great acting ability but very little knowledge of dance. Eventually we reached a satisfactory compromise whereby the boys received separate coaching in the basic rudiments of dance, and then struggled as best they could in the general classes.

They made remarkable progress this way, and once again I found their refreshingly light-hearted attitude towards ballet helped to prevent the rest of the group becoming bogged down by the mysteries of technique. The coaching classes were often hilarious, although the boys were more than willing to master the complexities of such an alien technique. What they lacked in finesse, they more than made up in enthusiasm.

They in return unwittingly taught me a great deal about the

art of teaching. Their constant questions on the reasons why you did certain exercises, and what they were for, made me thoroughly examine the practical results of accepted technical theories. From these questions, I began to understand what makes the basis of a sound, well-constructed class.

It was possible then to develop and extend theories of my own, knowing that they were a logical progression which would bear examination at a practical level. Many of these I discovered were in fact already an integral part of the Russian style of teaching. This was quite fascinating, as well as encouraging, for it confirmed my belief in the direction of my thoughts.

There are 'great teachers' just as there are 'great dancers'; after all without these teachers it would not be possible for the dancers to be successful. I became increasingly aware of how long it takes to develop the skills and craft of a teacher, as I continued to teach. It is really a lifetime's work, requiring years of experience dealing with people, before the qualities of a teacher begin to appear.

A dancer, however brilliant he may be, never feels there is nothing more to learn or improve. He returns to the classroom every day to correct and perfect the many steps and movements required for performance. So too, a teacher can never feel there is nothing else to discover about theory or technique. There is always something significant and new to be learned from observing a dancer's reactions and ability to cope with exercises.

The fascination of watching a dancer grow and develop in this way adds to the stimulus I never believed I would find through teaching. I had never considered I would have the patience to teach, being wildly impatient with my own imperfections as a dancer. Instead I find this impatience with myself makes me very sympathetic towards those I see struggling to master the same sort of problems.

It requires great tact and diplomacy, and a good understanding of human-nature to extract the right sort of reaction from each person, and I certainly do not profess to be successful in every instance! No two people, let alone two dancers, are the same, and their emotional make-up has to be taken into account if corrections are to be made and acted upon constructively. Even so, teachers and dancers need to have some common bond between them to create the best conditions for a successful communication.

I have not made any distinction between teaching in the classical style, as opposed to the modern style specifically, because basically the same principles apply to both. In many ways the only difference in teaching lies in the actual movements used. I know the major recognisable difference between modern, or contemporary dance, and ballet is usually based on the question of turn-out, but in many senses this is an immaterial factor.

The motivation for any dance training is the development of the body as a medium of expression. This in turn has to be governed by a strong discipline in order to establish the necessary control, and modern teachers are naturally as aware of this as those who teach classical.

I would always recommend that anyone wishing to train for modern, whether in the jazz, or Graham idiom, should first acquire some fundamental knowledge of the classical training. This is important because initially, classical provided the basis from which the other dance techniques were derived. I also think that some of the exercises used in ballet can demonstrate more forcibly to a person the muscle control and posture required for any other form of dance.

I think most modern teachers now also agree that an element of ballet training is very beneficial. Where they do have reservations is when fully trained classical dancers try to make the change over to modern dance without assessing the additional training that is necessary. What many classical dancers do not realise initially is that the approach to modern dance is completely differently orientated from that required for ballet.

Whereas ballet is based on an aspiration towards weightlessness and elevation, modern dance develops from a much more earthy quality, and is far more *terre à terre*. The transition from one to the other can therefore be very difficult. This is probably why some modern dance teachers are still wary of accepting, or advising students to train also in the classical style. But there is no reason why the use of one technique should not assist the other, as long as you are aware of this difficulty. It only remains then to discover which style best suits both your temperament and physique.

It is most rewarding as you begin to see results taking shape, but I find it difficult to imagine teaching without the fore-knowledge of performing oneself. It is after all the trials and tribulations of working on stage that eventually gives substance to the classwork. Usually a teacher without the experience of performing, can only teach the technique and practical application of the exercises. Initially this does not matter but, as a dancer begins to mature, an awareness of quality and presentation is needed to inspire the dancer to go beyond the technical require-ments of a ballet.

The rest of the work at the Coliseum was also extremely interesting, and gave me the opportunity of working with some marvellous people on the production side. I was also able to add to my knowledge of this side of the theatre, acting as assistant to the various choreographers who came to work with us. This, together with what I learned from producers about spacing and placing of people to create effective shapes on stage, began to give me an interest in doing some choreography myself. I was first given this opportunity by a producer friend, Tom Hawkes, whom I had met at the Coliseum.

He had been asked to do a production of *Carmen* in Southsea, and wanted me to arrange the dance in Act II. It was very good experience and I enjoyed it tremendously. I had only two dancers to work with for the greater part of the dance. This was enough for the size of the stage and the production, and also for me trying my hand at choreography for the first time! I also had to incorporate the three singing characters of Carmen, Frascita, and Mercedes at one point. This meant keeping their steps relatively simple, yet effective.

The two dancers had to mask any inadequacies on the singers' behalf and at the same time help to present these central figures in a flattering and prominent position. It was a good initiation for putting into practice the observations I had only been able to note mentally before. I was even more grateful then for the opportunities I had had, as an assistant to several of the most professional choreographers, before embarking on this sort of work myself. It could have been disastrous otherwise.

# II

## PRODUCTION OF A BALLET

### *Choreography, Design, Music and Notation*

AS A DANCER or actor, one is soon quick to admire, and distinguish between, the really professional and the rather less competent choreographers and producers in the theatre. It is a somewhat cruel, inborn characteristic of nearly all theatre people to be able to differentiate in a cold and clinical fashion the man who knows his job, and the one who is still floundering in a sea of insecurity.

It is more a critical faculty born out of instincts of self-preservation than anything else. A dancer can either wither or blossom artistically in the hands of a choreographer. If the former, certain defences have to be erected in time to prevent a complete depression of soul and spirit, whereas in the latter case one is able to relax, and even contribute something extra as well.

Experiences of this kind had taught me the amount of groundwork that is necessary before coming to rehearse with the dancers This groundwork is known literally as 'doing your homework', and in the long run can save hours of frustrated rehearsal time. A choreographer must know what he is aiming for, both stylistically and musically, long before starting work with the dancers.

Each choreographer works differently. Some have a very definite idea of the exact steps they want, others have only a vague idea of the whole shape. The ideas being suggested through the music and then finding a more exact interpretation worked out with the dancers during rehearsal.

All choreographers though are open to suggestion from the

dancers both through expressed ideas, or individually stylistic qualities. This close co-operation between dancer and choreographer is very important. A dancer's attitude of understanding and belief in the choreographer, and *vice versa*, ultimately produces a far richer end result. The combined efforts born out of a common sympathy for the work in hand achieves a much more satisfying and constructive ballet than can be realised otherwise.

To be able to read music is obviously a great asset, but even a very rudimentary knowledge can be sufficient. Together with a tape-recording of the particular piece of music being used, the score can be learned well ahead of rehearsals. Odd bars have to be clearly remembered, and the complexities they throw on the sequence of steps must be known well before actually reaching them in rehearsal so that you can guide both the accompanying pianist and the dancers.

A good pianist marks the score at various junctures with directions which he, as a non-dancer, can understand himself. this eliminates endless paging backwards and forwards through the score as rehearsals stop, start, and retrack over certain passages. This marking is invaluable and, when it comes to remounting a work at any time, these cryptic notes can provide an essential guide for whoever has to take rehearsals and remember the steps and their sequence.

In fact part of my job at the Coliseum was to make sure the score the Group used was appropriately marked up. In addition I also made my own notes of steps and pattern formations to facilitate rehearsals of revivals the following season. A good assistant can help a choreographer tremendously in this way for then there are no interminable delays as everyone racks their brains for the connecting links between steps. It also puts an end to the almost inevitable arguments amongst dancers, who doggedly stick to their memories of steps which often fail to coincide.

Another way the choreographer, or his assistant, can help towards the smooth running of rehearsals, is to block out clearly groups of four or eight bars on one side of a sheet of paper, with a brief note of steps and directions which take place during that time, written beside them. It makes for very easy reference in mid-rehearsal, and is a quick method of knowing how many bars from a certain point in a dance you need the pianist to begin, without constantly dashing over to the piano to look at the score. This is particularly so with a difficult score which initially is not easily absorbed in depth, even by the choreographer. These notes also act as an anchor amidst the turmoil of rehearsal when one seems to be thinking on four levels at once!

This sort of notation, and the method of lay-out is developed on a very personal and individual system, and is really only necessary when working with large groups and formations. *Pas de deux* are usually worked out with a pair of dancers in question on a more personal basis. Notation is a much more organised affair now than it used to be, and the above methods are rather frowned upon by the professional notators, or 'choreologists' as they are known.

Originally all works were handed down to future generations by word of mouth together with a series of rather imprecise notes and diagrams—much in the way I managed at the Coliseum. The disadvantage of this system is that one person's method of notating is very different from another's and often totally indecipherable by anyone other than the original author.

The symbols used by one person may mean quite the opposite to another reader. The literal translation of someone else's notes can be so frustrating and time-consuming, that it defeats the whole purpose of the original notes.

I still have books of notes taken at the Coliseum which are really valueless to anyone other than myself. I doubt if my dotted formations and directional arrows interspersed with graphically positioned pin-men would have helped my successor. Likewise the files I inherited from my predecessor caused more confusion and problems than help, as I used to peer at them during rehearsals, of a work with which I was still unfamiliar.

I am afraid to say that this is when dancers very often take full advantage of the situation. They know you cannot substantiate your deductions with any great authority, so small changes are subtly inserted to help them overcome their own particular problems.

The word of mouth method of handing down ballets, is equally unreliable. As I mentioned before, dancers anyway are renowned for each having their own interpretation and memories of individual steps, and even whole variations. This is understandable, especially at the soloist level, when individual interpretation is a very important part of presenting a role.

But it can be carried to extremes when the reasons for change are unwarranted. Gradually more and more inaccuracies appear, as each dancer overcomes a problem in his or her own way without supervision, and then passes on this new version to the next person.

The gravest danger of learning a ballet by word of mouth, is that very often the original conception is completely lost. The ballet becomes nothing more than an empty vehicle for a few unrelated solos, and *pas de deux*, and the *corps* work also suffers, ending up as a merely anonymous background. Most choreographers are naturally anxious to preserve the initial clarity of a presentation, and as long as they are still alive, or there is a deputy assistant who has worked closely by their side throughout the original creation, these defects can be corrected.

Either one of them can visit the Companies where the works are being presented. and clean up any inaccuracies before they become too firmly established. Even if ballets are not retained in their original entirety, at least there is a control over the adaptions made to suit new dancers. In this way the mood and shape of a ballet does not suffer. A change which has the authority of its creator, and is not devised by the dancer alone, is a very different matter from indiscriminate alterations.

A choreographer knows he has to recognise that there are always more ways than one of saying, or doing something, especially when he is dealing with individual people. By taking into account the physique and character of each individual dancer, he appreciates how best that particular dancer can portray a role. Once again a good assistant, who is attuned to the sensitivities of a choreographer, can be relied upon to make small changes which will not destroy the original idea.

The problem occurs when the choreographer or his assistant are no longer alive to preserve the ballet. Frequent changes creep in as dancers or producers seek to enhance sections of the ballet which have previously presented difficulties in one direction or another. It may be the dancer's fault again, or a producer feels adjustments are necessary to the *corps* arrangements to suit the available stage area.

Eventually a large proportion of the ballet is lost as memories of what really was the original, are buried beneath a mountain of additional material. This has happened in particular with classics like *Sleeping Beauty* and *Swan Lake*, which bear very little resemblance to the ballets as they were first performed.

Admittedly producers wishing to remount these particular works are not helped by the fact that Tchaikowsky wrote a vast amount of music for both ballets, a great deal of which it is not possible to place correctly in context. This is because, following the initial composition of the scores, Petipa arranged additional scenes and variations which required extra music. Consequently, producers now are faced with a wealth of music and possible 'variations on a theme'.

It must be remembered also that the capabilities of the dancers have developed tremendously since the end of the last century. Interesting as these works may be from an historic point of view, it is a shame not to keep them more up to date from a technical aspect. It is not only the abilities of the dancers which have improved, but also the facilities for lighting and other stage effects.

I think the majority of us would be very disappointed if we were to see these ballets now, as they must originally have appeared. They were far more of a spectacle then, presenting a lavish and glowing production based on a very slender fairy tale. Interpretation through actual dance was almost of secondary importance.

Closer to us in time are Fokine's ballets, such as *Les Sylphides* and *Petroushka* which may well be more successfully preserved. Fokine's ballet master was Serge Grigoriev, who married one of the Diaghilev ballerinas, Tchernicheva. She danced in many of Fokine's works and, when I was in the Company, we were fortunate enough to have the assistance of these two close associates of Fokine when we worked on any of his ballets.

They were both quite elderly then, but the life and vitality they showed in rehearsal was unbelievable. They were great perfectionists for detail, and would spend hours on just one scene to make sure it was as close to the original as possible, both in movement and especially in interpretation. It was amusing to note though, that even they would occasionally argue between themselves in Russian, as to the exact steps, or timing of a movement! Madame Grigorieva usually won, partly because she spoke better English than he did, and could therefore get her interpretation over better.

The Grigorievs' production at the Opera House are now recorded on film, but this does not lessen the feeling of loss due to their absence at rehearsals since the death of Monsieur Grigoriev.

Hopefully, more recent ballets will be even better preserved with the help of films, together with the more coherent forms of notation. I wonder too, whether perhaps there should not also be films of rehearsals in progress in order to capture the influence of the choreographer on points of interpretation and style. Although I personally feel that nothing can really replace the inspiring presence of the choreographer himself.

There are now two or three recognised forms of dance notation being taught, and a number of companies are already able to make use of the emerging choreologists—although it still takes another choreologist of the same school to translate the notation into actual dance steps. Usually a choreologist remains resident with one company. They notate new ballets as they are created, and act as an assistant to the choreographer during rehearsals. They also notate the current repertoire of the company, when not engaged on new work, and can take whole ballets over to other companies who wish to perform them.

The form of notation is usually based on principles similar to those used for music, and based on the stave. If you visualise a pin-man standing on the bottom line, the second line becomes his knees, the third his waist, the fourth his arms, with his head on the fifth. The pin-man is then reduced to a series of dots and dashes, depending on what he is doing.

The degree of success of this form of notation is still being argued among dancers. It appears to solve the problem and seems logical on the whole, although discrepancies in interpretation still arise. Recently a typewriter attachment has been evolved to record dance steps. So far this is proving very limited, but development of the idea could be useful in the future. Sometimes memory alone can serve as a better aid when remounting ballets, for the mind can remain open to suggestion, finding solutions based on reason. Dance notation tends to be rather more dogmatic ruling out the possibility of any variation from what is actually written down. This can create problems in rehearsals and arguments, as fierce as those engendered by the word-of-mouth method, are just as likely to flare up.

This does not mean I do not respect and admire the work done by choreologists. I recognise that it is a very valuable advance in the system of notating ballets, but I do feel there is still room for further development. It is interesting to note that in the eighteenth century even Noverre, known as the father of Modern Ballet, had already evolved a practical system of dance notation. It is still possible to get a very clear idea today of the ballets Noverre created, so long as one bears in mind the limitations and style of the dance technique as it existed then.

Of course notation has had to change in order to keep abreast of progress in dance techniques throughout the years. Even music today is beginning to have to make rather drastic changes in its methods of notation, to cope with the developments in scoring for electronic music. A score written by Cornelius Cardew, or John Cage bears little resemblance to the traditional forms of notation. So no one rigid law can really be laid down as to the best method or style of notation in dance. Each one is as transient as its predecessor, for it can only exist for the duration of its practicality.

The way in which a choreographer is inspired to create a ballet varies according to the individual, and it is very often a combination of sources of inspiration which sparks off the idea for a ballet. A book, a poem, a painting or a piece of music may all contribute to the beginning of an idea. Music is probably the most common single source of inspiration, for music can conjure up a very visual mental image.

Some pieces of music are already based on a specific theme or series of events to which the choreographer wishes to relate. More often though it is the abstract emotional nature of a score which captures the choreographer's imagination. Should the idea for a ballet stem from a more literary subject, the choreographer has then to find a suitable piece or pieces of music which will adapt to his requirements. Sometimes the two may occur almost simultaneously, then the fates seem to be very much on your side, especially if the literary source of inspiration happens to be of your own making.

Ideally a composer is commissioned to write a score for a ballet, in which case the choreographer and composer can work in close collaboration in order to achieve a very satisfactory and cohesive end result. It is unusual but not impossible for a choreographer to start choreographing a ballet before he has any music. In this case either the music is specially written by a composer who has great sympathy and understanding for the dance and dancers, or an electronically controlled score is arranged on tape-recordings which can be spliced and joined, and even synthesized if desired. This can also be done by the choreographer himself and indeed Alwin Nickolais is a very fine example.

There is an additional method of music-making which is based on improvision, whereby the dancers, through their movements provide the key to the instrumentalists' choice of musical interpretation, and *vice versa*. This sounds rather involved, but it is an experiment which is fascinating in its potential. In jazz music the musicians have a limited structure, within and from which they can expand and create depending on the moods and move-ments of their fellow players. It requires great understanding and involvement with the rest of the group, but the result can be extremely exciting, transcending the limits of one man's capa-bilities in composition.

This joint venture can be extended to include movement as well, as long as both the dancers and musicians are visually and aurally aware enough to react to each other. They are not left completely without direction though, nor do they improvise at the same time. There is the freedom for both dancers and musicians to express themselves through their own choice of movement, but the choreographer and composer have each provided the discipline of skeleton guide-lines, in order to keep the shape of the whole piece.

It is rather like seeing the bare structural elements of a building as conceived by an architect, and being allowed to use your own ideas to complete the external cladding; at all times bearing in mind the context within which it is arranged. This is unusual but certainly can be interesting. As yet the majority of this sort of co-ordination is confined to the more contemporary style dance, although there are of course similar experiments and de-velopments within the balletic field.

I do not feel traditional classical ballet lends itself very easily to this sort of interpretation though, for it does not maintain the contemporary qualities of the music. Classical ballet is developing in a contemporary sense, despite derogatory comments by its critics, but the pace of development is possibly not as advanced as in some other art forms. There are two reasons for this.

Firstly because it is still a relatively newly-discovered extension of the dance, the public has a tendency to cling to the now familiar tradition of the classics, and demands their constant presentation. This naturally limits a classical company's chance to progress as fast as it would wish. Secondly, there is the fact, as one dancer aptly put it, that until the body develops a few extra joints, a choreographer unlike other artists is really confined to using the same basic material without variations!

As I mentioned earlier another aspect which the choreographer must also consider when starting to work, is how his designer visualises the sets and costumes. Again a very close understanding of what each is trying to achieve is very necessary if they are to complement one another's work.

I was fortunate at the Coliseum in being asked to present a ballet project to the students of the Sadler's Wells Design Course, run by Miss Margaret Harris. Miss Harris, commonly known by the affectionate name of 'Percy', now works independently as a designer. She was part of 'Motley', the trio who together designed sets and costumes for many West End productions.

Working with these students, I came to understand how much a close collaboration can assist both designer and choreographer alike. In its way it is similar to the partnership between composer and choreographer. If the members of the creative team are in harmony, without changing the direction of the ballet as a whole, you sometimes finish up with a very different realisation of what you had originally intended, and the ballet really does become a joint project. It has germinated from the seed of one person's ideas to blossom and grow out of the close relationship and artistic understanding developed between two or three people.

I worked with the Design Course three years running. Each time it meant thoroughly preparing the subject matter, together with appropriate music, and being able to discuss the characters, their movements and the sort of setting required in some depth. It has been a very good way of discovering whether a project would work successfully in practice as well as in theory. Also working in close conjunction with each individual student, has proved to me how co-operation between the various contributors to a production can lead to a much more homogenous shape than if one sticks rigidly to preconceived ideas.

In fact I found all sorts of enlightening factors emerged from these discussions on possible interpretations. By giving the students almost total freedom to expand their own ideas I was often able to see how a ballet could take shape in a completely different and original form, yet still retain a traceable link with the basic concept. This experience has indirectly assisted me by helping to consolidate my ideas on teaching methods, albeit in a different medium, as well as stimulating an interest in choreography myself.

I stayed with the Coliseum for nearly two years, and enjoyed every minute of it. It helped to broaden my horizons considerably, but at the same time I knew the time had come for me to make a move. I had learned as much as I could in that particular sphere and, if I stayed on, there was a strong possibility of my settling into the complacency of a secure job, and not extending myself or my interests any further.

So by mutual consent Pauline Grant and I agreed to part. It was a hard and difficult wrench, for I had grown very fond of everyone there, but I am sure it was the right decision.

I have since been able to teach far more consistently, having discovered through being at the Coliseum, that that was where my interests really lay. Gary Cockrell at the Dance Centre in Floral Street, (just behind the Opera House) asked me if I would like to teach regularly at the Centre. I decided to take the plunge, and started teaching free-lance. It is a precarious business and I owe a great deal to Gary for his constant support both practical and moral. It is a slow business establishing a nucleus of a class, and one can become very disheartened by the length of time this takes.

The advantage of working freelance, of course, is that one is free to accept offers of other work as well. This has meant being able to work choreographically with Tom Hawkes again, and guest-teaching for a while with other ballet companies.

# 12

## RETURN TO THE ROYAL BALLET

### *Completing the Circle as Teacher and Repetiteuse*

I CERTAINLY DID NOT THINK when I started to write this book that I would finish up by joining the ends of a circle which was really set in motion when I joined the Royal Ballet. In a way, joining the Company is like becoming a member of a very large and diverse family. One remains fiercely loyal to it for the rest of one's career. And, as in a family, one may moan and groan about frustrations, even breaking away from it for a while, but always the sneaking desire is there to return and be accepted once more.

I was therefore extremely happy when after several discussions with Peter Wright (Co-Director of the Company), followed by my giving a trial class to some of the Company dancers, I was invited to return to the Royal as teacher to the 'New Group' which is in fact, a revised version and successor to the old Touring Company.

The welcome I received from the Company on my return was wonderfully warm. And after nervous pangs of doubt about whether I had made a wise decision, I knew that, for me, working with the Company again was really what I had always hoped would be possible, eventually. I had after all started teaching in order to give back some of the knowledge and experience I had gained as a dancer, and where better to do this than at the source of my own professional training?

The work is of course extremely rewarding, and the effort and concentration required are very worthwhile. By sheer coincidence

I was simultaneously asked by Norman Morrice, Director of Ballet Rambert, to teach with his Company. We came to an agreement between the two managements whereby I could teach Rambert once a week during the first month of working with the Royal. This I enjoyed immensely. It was also interesting from a teaching point of view, as one had to take into account the slightly different attitude required when teaching this more contemporary oriented company.

One thing I have become increasingly conscious of is that, as a teacher, one must remain constantly alert and aware of the flickering moods, tensions, and pressures under which one's pupils are working. This is essential if there is to be a constructive dialogue between you. The other levelling factor to remember also, is that you can never be omnipotent as a teacher and must accept that, for some dancers, you are not exactly the right person they need at that moment in their development. Like any relationship, the two parties do not necessarily complement each other all the time, or on every point.

This applies equally, of course, to the relationship between the teacher and a class of very individual dancers—not everyone is going to respond to the same degree. Once that can be expected and accepted the pleasure of one's work as a teacher, I have found, is enormous.

One of the other lovely things about coming back to work in the Company has been the pleasure of being in the theatre again. The excitement when new productions are being choreographed or re-mounted is infectious, and touring abroad still brightens the season. Suddenly the sublime conditions of working in an open-air amphitheatre, with a full-moon blazing overhead, makes it possible once again to face the grey English winters touring round the provinces.

And gradually, my work with the Company has developed beyond the classroom into the rehearsal period. Here both a knowledge of technique and the style of the ballet concerned are needed in order to coach dancers individually in solo and principal roles. Ballets like *Les Sylphides* which are particularly full of atmosphere, also need someone to rehearse the *corps* consistently, so that a uniformity of style as retained, as well as the essential *corps de ballet* precision.

This of course is an absorbing aspect of working with a Company and involves one far more with the actual production work. One can lay the guidelines and map out the motivation for the characters in a ballet, but each dancer has to weave his or her own individual talents and interpretation into the finished product. In this way it really becomes a joint effort brought about through a sympathy and understanding between two people, and to me the responsibility of helping individual dancers to realise their full potential is always an awe-inspiring venture.

In the meantime classes continue every day, on tour and off, while rehearsals crowd out the rest of the day. And always there is the perpetual cry of 'We need more time'!

★  ★  ★  ★  ★

As I write I am very conscious of the hard and grim picture I have possibly painted of the struggle it is to become a dancer, and having become one, how difficult it is to stay successfully within your chosen career. I hope you will not feel too down-hearted though, for the struggle can be a very worthwhile and rewarding one, and it is not for me to tell you how you should choose to live your life!

What I do hope I have done is to give you as clear and exact an impression as I can of the sort of existence most dancers lead, and to wish you luck if you decide to accept the challenge of this career, which is both pleasurable and painful. But at all times irresistible.

# APPENDIX

## *Where to Learn*

HERE IS A LIST OF SCHOOLS where dance and education are combined. They meet the requirements of the Department of Education and Science and, except where stated, all schools take both boys and girls.

**Art Educational Trust**   *Boarders* at Tring Park, Tring, Herts.
   *Day School* at Golden Lane House, Golden Lane, London EC1.

**Bush Davies Schools**   *Boarders* at Charters Towers, East Grinstead, Sussex.
   *Day School* at The Studio, 31 Eastern Road, Romford, Essex.

**The Elmhurst Ballet School**, Camberley, Surrey.
   *Boarders and Day Students* (Girls only), to diploma and G.C.E.
   With further stage training for up to two years.

**Grandison College,** 107 Park Lane, Croydon, Surrey.
   *Boarders and Day Students*

**The Hammond School,** Hampton Lodge, 12 Liverpool Road, Chester.
   *Junior School*—Boarders and Day Students to G.C.E.
   *Senior School*—continued stage training.

**The Italia Conti Stage School,** Avondale Hall, Landor Road, London, SW9.
   *Junior School*—9-16 years to G.C.E.
   *Senior School*—16-25 years continued stage training.

**The Legat School,** Mark Cross, Crowborough, East Sussex.
   *Boarders* to G.C.E.

**Pattison's Dancing Academy,** 86-90 Binley Road, Coventry.
   *Boarders and Day Students* to G.C.E.

**The Royal Ballet School**   *Junior School Boarders and Day Students*
11-16 years to G.C.E. at White Lodge, Richmond, Surrey.
*Senior School Day Students* (15 minimum, 17 maximum entry ages)
at 155 Talgarth Road, Barons Court, London W14.
Also at 155 Talgarth Road, *'Junior Associates'* part-time ballet only: 8-11 years.
and *Teachers Training Course* entry at 16 or over. Three year course.

**The Stella Mann School,** 343a Finchley Road, London NW3.
*Junior School*—10-16 years to G.C.E.
*Senior School*—16 years minimum entry age—continued stage training.
Also part-time courses for adults and children after school hours.

★ ★ ★ ★ ★

The following are Schools of Contemporary Dance and Ballet only. They have
no educational facilities, but classes are arranged so that they fit in with ordinary
school hours.

**The Andrew Hardie School of Dancing,** 17 Queensbury Mews West,
London SW7.
Age 6 years and upwards to Senior Students (Ballet)

**The Ballairs School of Dance and Drama,** Millbrook, Mill Lane, Guildford,
Surrey.
*Senior School* (after G.C.E.), full comprehensive stage training

**The Dance Centre,** 12 Floral Street, London WC2 (just behind the Royal
Opera House, Covent Garden).
Open classes at all levels, for both adults and children in classical,
modern, jazz, tap, *pas de deux* and yoga.
Details and class time-tables on application.

**The Place,** full details from 17 Duke's Road, London WC1.
Mainly contemporary dance, Graham style. A full-time dance
course including some ballet, also open classes for senior students and
professionals from beginners level upwards.
*The Place* also has its own cinema, theatre and restaurant.

**The Rambert School of Ballet** at The Mercury Theatre, 2 Ladbroke Road,
London W11.
*Junior School,* classes after school hours for children from four years old.
*Senior School* (after G.C.E.), fully comprehensive stage training.

**The Royal Academy of Dancing,** 48 Vicarage Crescent, Battersea, London
  SW11.
*Scholarship courses* for children all over England.
Classes arranged by teachers authorised by the Academy, following
selection by audition for successful candidates.
*Teachers Training courses.* Entry at age 16 or over. Three year course,
with diploma on completion. Five G.C.E. 'O' levels or equivalent
required as part of entry conditions.

**The Ruth French School of Ballet,** 155a Kings Road, Chelsea, London SW3.
Adults and children (Ballet).

This is only a selection of some of the better-known schools. There are also
many others. Extensive lists of reputable schools are published in the *Dancing
Times* under 'Where to Learn'. A number of schools also advertise in the
*Dancing Times* and in *Dance and Dancers*, the two major dance magazines in
England.

Another fund of information is John O'Brien's bookshop in Cecil Court,
just off St. Martins Lane, London. He stocks books on every aspect of the dance
world as well as the cinema and theatre. Magazines include copies of English,
French and American editions, which can be very helpful when you are searching for information about foreign companies with regard to possible employment.

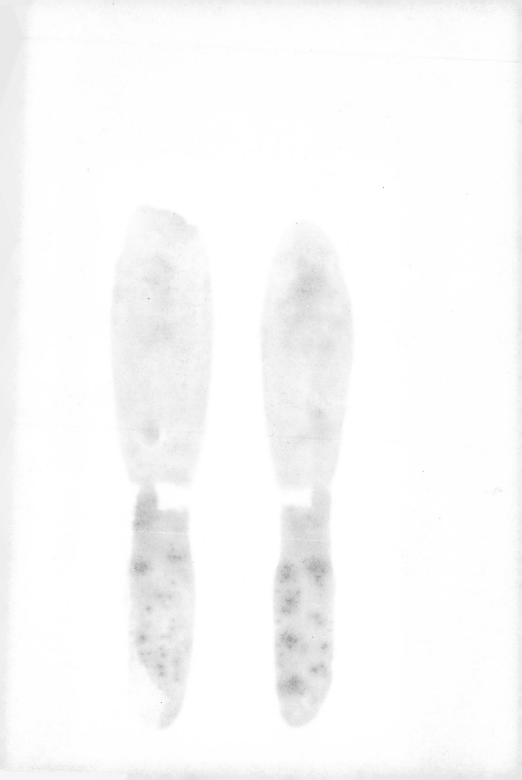

## DATE DUE

GAYLORD                    PRINTED IN U.S.A.

## DATE DUE

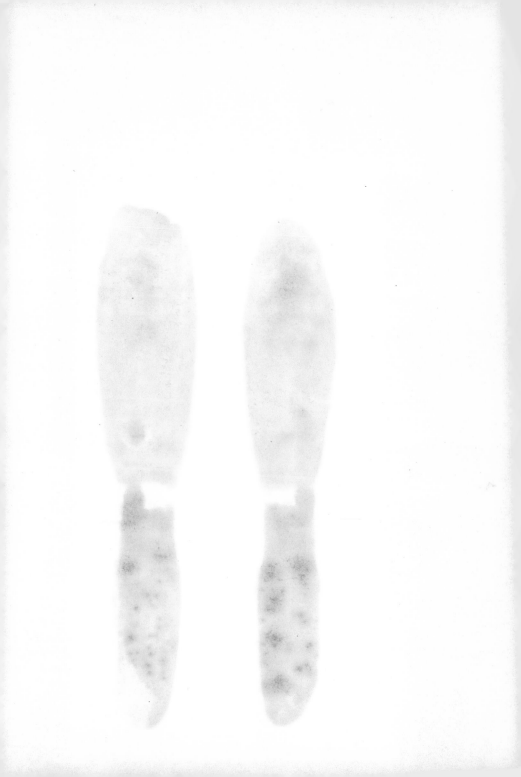